DATE DUE

JUN 1 2 2008	
JUL 0 1 2008	
AUG 0 1 2008	
AUG 1 8 2008	
SEP 0 8 2008	
OCT 1 4 2008	
AUG 1 1 2010	
AUG 2 3 2010	
SEP 1 0 2010	
FEB 0 7 2012	
DEC 2 0 2018	

DEMCO, INC. 38-2931

D1377794

WRITING ON STONE

WRITING ON STONE

Scenes from a Maine Island Life

Christina Marsden Gillis

Photographs by Peter Ralston
With a Foreword by Philip Conkling

University Press of New England
Hanover and London
and
Island Institute
Rockland, Maine

Island Institute
Published by University Press of New England,
One Court Street, Lebanon, NH 03766
www.upne.com
© 2008 by University Press of New England
Printed in the United States of America
5 4 3 2 1

Library of Congress Cataloging-in-Publication Data

Gillis, Christina Marsden
  Writing on stone: scenes from a Maine island life / Christina Marsden Gillis;
photographs by Peter Ralston; with a foreword by Philip Conkling.
  p. cm.
ISBN-13: 978–1–58465–697–5 (cloth : alk. paper)
ISBN-10: 1–58465–697–2 (cloth : alk. paper)
1. Great Gott Island (Me.)—Social life and customs. 2. Great Gott Island(Me.)—Biography.
3. Gillis, Christina Marsden. 4. Gillis, Christina Marsden—Family. 5. Gillis, Benjamin Robert,
1965–1991—Death and burial. 6. Sons—Maine—Great Gott Island—Death. 7. Sepulchral
monuments—Maine—Great Gott Island. 8. Great Gott Island (Me.)—Description and travel.
9. Great Gott Island (Me.)—Pictoral works. I.Title.
  F29.H3G55 2008
  974.1'45—dc22
  [B]   2007044804

Designed and typeset by Bridget Leavitt, Island Institute

Brief excerpts as submitted from "Phebe Bunker", "The Ghost of Phebe Bunker", and "Time to Go" from TIME'S WEB by RUTH MOORE. COPYRIGHT©1972 by RUTH MOORE. Reprinted by permission of HarperCollins Publishers WILLIAM MORROW.

For Ben

CONTENTS

FOREWORD

I first met Christina Gillis at an "Islands of the Mind" Conference she helped host at Rutgers University in May 2004. I don't know what I was expecting from a meeting of island academics from around the world, except I was totally shocked to encounter someone for whom the memory of islands was written so deeply into her being. During a time meant for small talk prior to dinner for the participants, she said she was struck by the use of a phrase, "cellar hole melancholy," I had quoted in the essay I was to present describing how Maine islanders refer to feeling that their memories seep out of every inch of their native ground. She said she knew that feeling.

At the end of the conference, Tina told me she was working on a piece of writing that she would send me when it was published. When I read her essay, "Foundation," on which this book is based, my heart nearly stopped. Her writing takes us to places at once completely "en-isled," and deeply connected to both past and future. Such transcendent writing makes you feel something fundamental move under your feet and you hear the wind rushing in your ears.

If, as Goethe wrote, the shock of recognition runs the world round, may you recognize something of your life, your spirit, in these pages.

Philip Conkling
Founder, Island Institute

ACKNOWLEDGMENTS

First and foremost, to John Gillis, goes my fondest appreciation: for his broad knowledge of islands and islandness, for his support and encouragement of this book, and for shared experience of life and loss, on island and mainland, over more than four decades. As each new generation brings something special to the island, so too I thank our son Christopher Gillis, his wife, Kathy Armstrong, and their children, Peter and Astrid, who show us what is still new about a place we think we know so well. No less valuable was the help of my parents, Robert and Nan Marsden, who made possible our acquiring the house at Gotts Island and then, through the untimely death of my father, were unable to enjoy it together with us. This book would not have been written, my island life not lived, if my sister, Phyllis Strauss Paradis, had not invited us to Gotts Island so many years ago. In Phyllis's Massachusetts living room, at about age ten, I first heard of the remote place named Gotts Island that was later to mean so much in my life. Our friends Lance and Marjorie Farrar, as well as countless other visitors to the island, brought us wine and fresh vegetables, but even more important, they gave us the opportunity to share a special place. Those with whom we most actively share the island, of course, are our neighbors. Over the years I traverse in this book, the other Gotts Islanders, some named, some not, have all contributed in ways they may not even know. They are the human fabric of the island. It is impossible to think about Gotts Island, let alone write about it, without them. Of those named, Northwood Kenway, and his wife, Rita, have been our closest neighbors for all the years we have been on the island; literally and figuratively, they are the center of the old village.

Encouragement and support have come from other sources as well. In Berkeley, Nellie Hill, Victoria Nelson, Lynne Knight, Harvey and Rhona Weinstein, Jayne Walker, David Reid, and Marjorie Fletcher have offered critique and confirmation at various stages of this project. At their ever welcoming dining table, in Berkeley and in London, David and Mary Alice Lowenthal have provided wonderful occasions for good and inspiring talk about islands. Beth Dungan has been my valuable partner in countless conversations and presentations, generously bringing her deep knowledge of the visual arts to bear on issues of death and dying where words alone can be inadequate. I was fortunate to share a short, early piece on the island with my fellow members of the "Life and Death" potluck discussion group, which, under the gentle and wise guidance of Guy Micco, has for more than fourteen years covered a vast territory of ideas on death and dying. Paul Alpers, Sandra Gilbert, Robert and Micha Grudin, Charles Muscatine, and Alex Zwerdling, provided valuable affirmation, as, further afield, did Scott and Kay Armstrong, Albert LaFarge, Adam Nicolson, and Clifford Earl Ramsey. Even further, my thanks to Kenzaburo Oe, who visited Berkeley on a memorable occasion, talked with me about loss (and return), and sent me a copy of his Nobel acceptance lecture with a moving note that came to mean so much. Thanks go too to Elaine Greene, who asked all the right questions and published my first piece on Gotts Island in her "Thoughts of Home" section of *House Beautiful*; to Jackson Lears and *Raritan* for publishing "Foundation"; to Philip Conkling and David Platt for re-publishing "Foundation" in *Island Journal*; and to Island Institute co-founder Peter Ralston, whose photography is a gift to any writer. I am privileged to have Peter's work in the book. If my language can approach the rhetorical power of his images, I will have succeeded indeed.

The Island Institute has played an especially important role in the story of this book. I am deeply grateful to Philip Conkling, David Platt, and Peter Ralston for their active role in its production; for their commitment to the life of the Maine islands; and for encouraging me to believe that, though living most of the year in California, I too am a Maine writer.

Finally, to Phyllis Deutsch and her colleagues at the University Press of New England, a very special thanks for bringing this book, and a small island, to a larger world.

WRITING ON STONE

1

TO THE ISLAND

Prologue

In 1789, Daniel Gott, descendant of a large family that had settled originally around Gloucester, Massachusetts, acquired a small island off the southwest edge of what is now Mount Desert Island, Maine. Of the settlement that Daniel Gott established on the island, little now remains. "Less than two hundred years was their time here/Theirs and their sons/Who now are names in stone," the writer Ruth Moore, born on the island to one of its earliest families, would write in a poem published in 1972. Gotts Island had, in her view, disappeared; the memory of the life that had flourished there was now frozen in stone.

On December 26, 1991, at the Masai Mara game preserve in Kenya, when it was still Christmas Day at our home in Berkeley, California, our son Ben was killed flying a small plane from Mombassa to Little Governors Camp. Seven months later, in July 1992, we buried Ben's ashes in the cemetery at Gotts Island, where our family had summered for almost forty years. We marked the grave with a simple flat oblong piece of granite. Ben became a "name in stone."

There is no story here, no narrative, no real explanation of this death. Ben had gone out to Kenya because he loved to fly and wanted to see and participate in another world. He was killed by a large bird that just happened to be in his flight path, near Little Governors camp in the Masai

Mara, which we had ourselves visited two years before. This was surely a bizarre death. The bird came through the windscreen of Ben's plane, killing him instantly. The plane went down and burst into flames. The eight passengers, all European tourists whose names I do not know, died in the flames. They too must have had families. But I will never know those people, even though I share a terrible bond with them.

This is an accidental death, fundamentally inexplicable. It marks the point between the before and after in our lives. Ben's grave in the island cemetery, a small, bounded and fenced place at the center of what was once the island village, is the physical marker of that crucial temporal divide. We can know loss but we may never know why it occurs. We seek consolation, then, for what has been lost but also for our not knowing. Children are not supposed to die before their parents; they are supposed to carry on the memory—of their own lives and of those of the generation that precedes them. They are supposed to keep the story, to explain to their children the family photographs that pile up in the cabinet or drawer. The child's death, the unnatural, unanticipated event, seems, in our darkest moments, to truncate our own future.

But with the horror and enigma of accidental death comes also the urge to accommodate the past and the present, the gains as well as the losses. Gotts Island, a place of stone remnants, is a space of accommodation. And there is consolation in that. The island, sparkling and bright on a beautiful day in July, alive with summertime voices, is at the same time a site of loss, of physical deterioration, of the fragility of the structures that we and our antecedents have built. Its story is one of human forces, of economic and demographic change. Like so many of its Atlantic counterparts, the island is marked literally by a process of depopulation that dominated its history in the early decades of the twentieth century. This is the central drama that unfolded against the magnificent backdrop of sea, land, and granite. The place and its story are integral each to the other.

We tend to think of place in terms of location, fixity. "Time and place," we say, as if the two were entirely separate. But removed from time, place tells us so little. In an aerial photograph taken in 1956, Great Gott, with three neighboring islands, floats amoeba-like in a black sea. Each of the islands is dominated by heavy spruce forests, dark gray splotches sparsely punctuated by small light patches of open land. Around each, but most noticeable on Great Gott, a bright rocky belt stands out in sharp relief against the darkness of the sea. Gotts, a mile across and three miles around, is irregular, almost unruly, a large bulbous shape attached by a narrow neck to a much smaller bulge at its eastern headland. But the boundaries ringed with bright granite appear to keep the island in place, secure, firm, and unchanging within the sea that commands most of the photographic space. Ruth Moore emphasized the independence of the small land mass when she wrote that the offshore islands "belong to themselves/They stand in their own sea"; but the photograph suggests relationships as well: island to island, dark forest to bright inhabited patch, minute building to broad and expansive surround of island studded sea.

Signs of the human are hard to find in the aerial image. No lobster boats ply that water; no island paths or tracks are visible. The caption on the photograph tells me that the existing buildings on Great Gott "show clearly . . . most of them dating from the nineteenth century." But I cannot see those buildings. Only with the help of a magnifying glass will I find my own house, a mere speck joining the others in the lighter space just to the west of the irregular dark that dominates the island.

The stillness, the static quality, of the 1956 aerial photo of the island leaves out the story of change. It leaves out history, patterns that in large measure explain the dominance of the dark spruce and sparseness of habitation. Before the forest in the aerial photograph, before the landscape that we know, was the nineteenth-century village. A few houses, like my own, remain. They sit squarely on their foundations of local granite blocks. These are the houses of the living, of the present. Sparse stony traces, mere rectangles, are all that remain of the village of the absent. We live in juxtaposition to the traces, and yet, we are always surprised to come upon foundations half buried in "seas of spruces"; within the density and gloom, it is hard to imagine that an open sheep pasture once existed there.

"Less than two hundred years was their time here": Moore placed a time frame around the original island community that began in the eighteenth century but could not survive the twentieth. Like the photograph, she too suggests fixity, boundedness in time: what is gone is gone.

But ever mindful of the world that was lost, we see the island as our place too. The summer people, the "rusticators," were already coming when Ruth Moore was a young girl in the first decade of the twentieth century; her family took them in as boarders. Ultimately, the summer people moved into the few remaining village houses, gradually repaired the roofs, walls, and windows, stopped the leaks, tried to beat back the ever encroaching spruce. We brought our books, our projects, our lives. Our children would return with us each summer with another year's growth. In our family photograph collection two small blond boys in high-top overalls staring into the late afternoon sun from the front deck of the house turn into two shirtless adolescents working on the rough turf of the front yard with lawnmower and rake.

The island culture that never completely disappeared, the stuff of memory and story, reflects and refracts our family's history of personal loss. For me, the two stories speak to one another in a dialogue that is oddly sustaining. I live in the house once owned by Ruth Moore, who made the process of depopulation and departure a major theme in her poetry and fiction. Ruth knew all too well the progression from discouragement, to the moss-covered roof of an abandoned house, to the empty foundation space. Her own family were among those who left, and in the 1960s she sold off the last of the Moores' Gotts Island property. Perhaps, having re-created the island in her larger narrative of loss, she no longer needed the place itself.

Ruth Moore's house, my house, is a place of ghosts, voices, material objects—all simulacra of lives and histories, those of our own family, those that long preceded us. Past and present seem to flow into one another. After Ben's death, representation itself took on new meaning. Moore's fictive view of a culture that disappeared, though not necessarily mine, is so immediate, so close.

In leaving out time and history, in depicting the island as complete and intact, the aerial photo also leaves out narrative and the role that we ourselves play in constructing it. What appears as a clearly identifiable piece of land, a contained and supposed known, is also a place of the incomplete, the contingent, where the past still holds its power and fragments remind us of everything we will never know. The island is a place where emptiness reverberates through barren rock, fields of wet grasses, empty foundations, straggling walls that go nowhere, flint-gray sea. To read the island as a place is to recognize that facts alone cannot explain or describe such loss. We must account for and value the fragments of the absent: the graves in the cemetery, the fence post that once marked a pasture now buried in moss and spruce, the stones that mark the foundations of houses long gone.

The island, revisited again and again, is never entirely fixed. Place tells in its own particular way; it enables us to incorporate into our lives and into our language those we have lost and those with whom we still share the living community. A process of active making transforms absence, takes up the pieces—shards of memory, stories, experiences—and re-forms them into a coherent pattern. Memory is self-affirming—we are what we remember—but it also engages us in a dynamic relationship with the place that makes the memory possible.

Maine writer and environmentalist Philip Conkling tells us that smooth round rocks called "popplestones" were collected by late eighteenth-century Maine islanders to ballast the holds of homemade sailing vessels. Later they were used to pave the streets of East Coast cities. Stories, reminiscences, old myths, and present meditations are my popplestones. They are my building materials. They enable me to give shape to the island, to experience, to small incidents that are remembered in odd ways.

The contained space of Ben's gravesite, the stone as marker, is central to the story I want to tell, the structure I want to fabricate. That modest rectangular stone is linked to the fenced ground of the cemetery that was once the heart of the village and is still a kind of center for the summer residents. The cemetery is a place where people go. We may go there to read the stones and think about lives past, people whose stories we have heard and whose names identify some of the still-standing houses; we may go there simply because, in midsummer, it's the best place to view the sunset. The important point is that the island cemetery is fully integrated into its surround. Though importantly bounded by its fence, it shares the field with the annual Fourth of July softball game.

Neither the stone marker nor the fenced cemetery is ultimately islanded from the land each occupies. Coterminous with the rockbound belt of the island itself, each is an island within an island, each crystallizing and intensifying experience, containing and concentrating it such that the connections are more knowable. A locus of supposed loss becomes a place of connected structures, places, people, history: a place of life.

These structures are not viewable in a static photo. We can know them only with arrival, and repeated arrivals, at the island itself. We come back each year to traverse the rocks, follow the paths, read the stones, inhabit the space. We revisit, yet again, the island that belongs, yes, to itself, but also to us.

Getting There

So how far back do I go in explaining how our family came to Gotts Island? After all, none of us summer people would be there if the island population had not succumbed to economic and social stress, if the coast of Maine had not turned into a summer "destination," if the American middle class had not come to value the summer house as a family space, connected ideally with nature or a past available to nostalgic longing.

But these factors, even if true, are too remote. I got to Gotts Island because at the end of World War II, my sister Phyllis, twenty years older than I, married into a Philadelphia family named Strauss who had vacationed in Maine first as summer boarders and then, in the 1940s, as owners of a house at Gotts Island. I was eleven when I made my first trip to the island, visiting my grown-up sister, who by then had three small children and was living in the Strausses' rambling arts and craft–style log cabin sited beside the granite rocks and the sea. I have only a dim recollection of that summer, of the multi-leveled rustic house with a large granite outcropping forming the dining room wall, of the omnipresent sound of ocean and rock. After that visit I never saw the house again. A decade later, it burned to the ground; only the granite wall remains.

It was 1963 when I next visited my sister at Gotts Island. By now I was married and the mother of a four-month-old infant, and my sister and her husband Richard had bought the old Moore family house, built in the mid-nineteenth century by one of Daniel Gott's great grandsons and virtually abandoned when the permanent community left in the late 1920s. The house had suffered seriously over the years.

My sister had valiantly begun several rehab projects, but only two rooms had ceilings that did not rain plaster on our heads. A few tattered traces of elegant wallpaper in the front hall of the main house served as small reminders of what the house must have been in its earlier days.

That summer, my husband, John, and I had just arrived from California, where he was a graduate student, and we were on our way to spend a year of dissertation research in Germany. In our week with Phyllis and her family we noticed a note tacked up in the Gotts Island mail shack to which Russell Gott dutifully delivered the mail each day. Elling Aannestad, who owned the small house dubbed "box on the rocks" at the far eastern edge of the island, planned to spend the next summer in Europe and wanted to rent out his house. There was no fixed time; the rent was $250 for as long as one wanted to stay. We knew we would need an inexpensive place to stay the next summer when we returned from Europe. We knew the island was a place we wanted to be. With little hesitation we signed on to rent Elling's "box on the rocks" for the entire summer of 1964.

Thus we embarked on the first episode of what would become a ritual of spending at least part of every summer at the island. That first summer, we lived literally on the granite ledges. The sea pounded in almost at our front door; immediately behind us were the empty foundation stones of Miss Peterson's house, well known in island lore as the structure that had burned to the ground in the 1920s.

Sorting through forty years of family correspondence and photos in the summer of 2004, I came upon the letter my father wrote in the spring of 1965 informing John and me that if we would contribute $2000, he would put up $5000 to buy the Moore house from my sister and brother-in-law. Tired of dealing with the problems of a house that still suffered the ills of years of neglect, Phyllis and Richard had just purchased another piece of property from Ruth Moore, this one with shorefront, and planned to build a brand new house close to the water. For $7000, the old house became ours. We acquired a six-bedroom structure complete with barn and store, eleven acres, and a view that may be unsurpassed anywhere in the state of Maine. And, of course, we also acquired the leaky roof, cracked and falling plaster, a "water system" that consisted of a cistern in the basement to catch the roof run-off, a woodstove as the sole cooking facility, kerosene and candles as the only source of light.

The year 1965 turned out to be a major transition point in our lives. John finished his Ph.D. and accepted a teaching job in the East, our son Chris was now two, and we were expecting another baby. Two months after signing the deal to purchase the Gotts Island house, we drove east, visited my parents at their home in Rhode Island, and continued on to the island to spend the rest of the summer in our newly acquired house. We were young, and things were happening very fast for us. I'm not sure we appreciated the large challenge we had just taken on. Certainly we had no notion of the role this house was to play in our future.

In our brief time in Rhode Island it had been clear that my father was not well; but as ever in our family, no one took illness seriously and everyone spoke cheerfully of my parents' coming up to join us at the island as soon as they could—this despite the fact that my father, a lifelong smoker, was having serious difficulty breathing and there were quiet allusions to heart dysfunction. Saying good-bye to him on a July morning, I had a terrible premonition that this was farewell indeed. I couldn't rid myself of this idea throughout the long, hot drive to Maine. We were embarked upon a kind of new beginning, but the notion of ending and loss hung about me like a dead weight.

The phone call informing us of my father's death came in to HG Reed's Store in Bass Harbor on the second night we were on the island. No one goes to Gotts Island in the dark and at low tide. No one on the island had a telephone at that time. The message, the note on the piece of paper, had to be delivered early the next morning, on the high tide, by one of the local fishermen. My sister got the news first: my father's breathing difficulties had worsened and his heart had given out the preceding evening in a Providence hospital. John and I were still asleep when my sister came into the house to tell us.

I was twenty-six that summer, six months pregnant with the child who would spend all the summers of his childhood at Gotts Island and would die twenty-six years later on a savannah in East Africa. Again we would be awakened, this time by a phone call in California, and the news would come from a place far distant from Maine; but six months later, when that place was inscribed on a granite stone in the island cemetery, we learned that physical distance meant little. That place on the other side of the world had become inextricably linked to a small island's much larger story.

2

DOCKING

Voyage

Our destination on this June day is the dock at the island, but this visit, like the forty odd that have preceded it, begins with the voyage out. No matter that the trip from the mainland, even in bad weather, takes less than half an hour; or that this classic odyssey will terminate ultimately in a return to Bass Harbor and the car parked in the lot operated by the Maine State Ferry Service. This journey, however brief, will carry us, at least in imagination, from one world to another. The voyage to Great Gott Island, two miles off the tip of Mount Desert Island in Blue Hill Bay, is no exception to a pattern that can rightly be called mythic.

But I am more interested in the domestication of myth. The so-called eternal return concerns me less than the experience of arrival—complete with bags, bundles, books, and equipment. Now we have stowed our gear and ourselves into Lyford Stanley's boat; we have passed the Swan's Island Ferry dock and the sailing yachts sitting sedately at anchor just beyond it; we have moved out to the south, toward the Bass Harbor light and the clanging bell buoy in the channel between the mainland and Gotts Island. Here in the Westward Way, we have felt the swell in the sea when the tide is running counter to the wind.

Once in the channel we see our destination clearly. The island lies straight ahead. Soon we will be passing the meadow at its northwestern tip. The outboard motor whirs on, propelling us on a course roughly parallel to Gotts' mainly wooded western shore, moving us toward the bar that juts out in embrace of the middle and inner pools. Lyford keeps the boat ever parallel to the shore but far enough out to clear the bar, far enough to bring suddenly into view the village houses and the white-fenced cemetery that stud the hillside.

We round the end of the bar, feel the pull of the tide between Gotts and its small twin, Little Gotts, and enter the outer pool at high water. The sharply pitched roof of Uncle Mont Gott's old red cottage is now before us, still keeping watch on the pool and the dock more than forty years after the death of its last, solitary, year-round resident.

As Lyford slows the outboard and maneuvers among the increasing number of moorings in the pool, we get ready to gather up our bags and assorted bundles; it's time to disembark. The dock awaits the arrival that will be also a beginning. What will be begun, what ended, what learned or even unlearned, is still shrouded from view, as if secreted within the island itself. But we have come to the place of entry. Lyford cruises in to the dock and ties up the boat. We have landed.

At the Dock

"How long are you on for?"

As I step on to the dock it sways and wobbles slightly in high water. A neighbor tying up his boat has asked the expected question; his query reminds me that as soon as l set foot on the shore of the island, I am "on." I will step into my island self. But for a brief moment, here on the dock, lifting bags and boxes from the boat, fussing with gear, I am in a borderland between the then and the now, there and here, "off" and "on."

Usable only about two hours before and two hours after high water, the dock is a modest enough affair in no way comparable to the actual role it plays. On an island, arrival, departure, the greeting of friends, the reception of materials and supplies, the exchange of news or gossip—to paraphrase the old Simon and Garfunkle song, it's all happening at the dock. Never entirely fixed, our gauge of time and tide, the dock reflects the pace of life on the island. At low tide, with the pool an empty expanse of mud and stones, when the float sits inertly on the pebbly, shell-strewn ooze, the island falls into a lull, as if left to itself, to contemplation, to chores, to life that does not extend far beyond itself. It seems to wait for the incoming tide that will enable the dock to float and become once again the connecting point with the mainland.

Then, especially when high water coincides with midday hours, comes the noticeable flurry of activity: "We have to catch the tide," we say. I hear the sound of Lyford Stanley's four-wheeler helping a family lug their gear to a cottage half a mile away down the town road; I see neighbors with fishing rods heading to their skiffs in the pool; I see others, more athletically inclined, intent on rowing out and around Little Gotts Island or even further out; I hear the high-pitched voices of the small children, laden with towels and beach paraphernalia, on their way down to paddle in the water that now, at last, has filled up the pool by the dock. On a warm day, this is the time I get into a bathing suit myself and walk down to brave the cold water.

No one place on the island reveals time and change more than the dock and the area around it. The shore at Gotts Island now bears little or no resemblance to what we would have found a century ago when it was a "working waterfront," a place that to the modern eye would seem a disordered jumble of tubs, barrels, crates, and assorted gear. Upon arriving at a Maine offshore island, the protagonist in one of Sarah Orne Jewett's tales is dismayed to find "a litter of drift-wood, of dilapidated boats and empty barrels and broken lobster pots, and a little higher on the shore . . . a tar kettle." Contemporary summer visitors would find the working waterfront at best unsightly and at worst despicable. We are uncomfortable if an unwary islander leaves a bucket of bait on the dock; it just doesn't belong there. The dock should be pristine, empty.

For our nineteenth-century island forebears who worked the sea, renewal and repair meant literally that: life was a struggle to keep at bay the unremitting processes of disintegration inflicted by nature and fate. Signs of that disintegration, and of repair, would be everywhere. The dock and the waterfront were sites where livings were eked out of the sea; the stories of struggle and loss that took place there—dramas we can read in the Gotts Island cemetery—take on, in retrospect, heroic dimensions, at odds with our own more mundane work lives, our mainland lives.

For us, the summer people, the clean, empty dock is a stage, still perhaps a place for re-creation and renewal, but now for recreating or renewing ourselves. A visitor who arrived at the island on a day of dense fog remarked that he felt he was moving on a stage set. He couldn't see an edge, he couldn't see beyond the fog to any other space, real or imagined. He could only await the next scene.

But we are transient characters. Making our entrances and exits at the dock, we are, Maine writer George Putz has said, "protagonists in our own stories." The dock is for us an open-ended space, a space of transformation. Social relations are formed, and observed, at the dock. Facts, gossip—a certain kind of knowledge is exchanged there. But the larger dramas, of experience and loss, of what cannot be learned as fact or gossip, also begin at the dock. And for them, there is neither denouement nor resolution. Journeys or quests begun at the landing place may lead to knowledge that is only partial at best; far better to value the journey, the enactment, narrative itself.

Impressions

On a brilliantly clear day in July 1992 we climbed out of
a green motorboat and hauled on to the Gotts Island dock
the flat oblong stone we had ordered the month before for
Ben's grave. In a sense it was the ending of a journey that
had begun in Africa, or perhaps even long before that. But
naming a beginning or an ending was not the point. Our
story had no real completion; nor was explanation, in the
usual sense of the term, necessary. Ritual provides its own
story, tracing on the land its own kind of knowledge.

"In cases of fatal accident abroad, we recommend cremating
the body in the country where the death occurred rather
than sending it home," the kind but matter of fact voice on
the telephone from the American consulate in Nairobi told
us. The message was all too clear. The corporeal remains of
our son, *qua* body, were gone from us. Instead, we would
have a small, discreetly sealed, cedar box of ashes, a talis-
man for a young, vibrant life that has been lost. The box
would travel from Nairobi, via London, to Philadelphia;
then to California; and finally back to the East Coast for
burial in the place where Ben had spent at least a part of the
twenty-six summers of his life.

As advised by the consulate, Ben's body was cremated by
Hindus in Nairobi. His friend Michelle, who had at age
twenty-four overseen the arrangements there, had—I
would later learn—lit the funeral pyre, brought the ashes
home in a small cedar box which she handed to John, Chris,
and me in the bar of a hotel at the Philadelphia airport. Very
soon thereafter, Northwood Kenway, in his role as manager

of the island cemetery, kindly invited us to bury Ben's ashes there.

We wanted Maine granite for Ben's stone. We envisioned stone that would be rose pink like the rocks by the inner pool when the tide is out late in the day. But when we arrived in Ellsworth on a gray day in June 1992 to purchase the stone, Mrs. Dunn, who ran the business, explained to us that they were no longer quarrying that granite locally; we would have to use Vermont stone.

We walked among the stones laid out like a phantom cemetery in the back yard of Mrs. Dunn's shop, a small house on a quiet side street. Mrs. Dunn and her daughter had been well recommended to us. They provided and engraved the stones for E. B. White, for Paul DeMan, and for Jimmy Kenway, Northwood and Rita's son who was killed at age thirty-five in a ski accident at Killington, Vermont. We chose a stone that was only slightly rose. But it was not gray and it was not white. Mrs. Dunn would see that it was properly engraved.

Three days before we planned to bury Ben's ashes in the island cemetery, Chris, John, and I brought the stone to the island. We had chosen well. The granite seemed to glow with a soft light of its own as we performed a strange and unfamiliar task: carrying a gravestone from the car parked on the ferry dock at Bass Harbor, past the vacationers waiting to board an island cruise excursion, and down the ramp to the waiting boat. No one commented at the sight of three people carrying a gravestone to a small motorboat. It was another piece of baggage going out to the island;

we made space for it among Chris's luggage and the inevitable groceries just purchased at Doug's Shop 'n Save in
Ellsworth. All days off the island have to be used well, all
the necessary errands accomplished. Even ritualized tasks
are, after all, tasks.

I still see clearly in memory our arrival at the Gotts Island dock that day. I see Chris and John straining to lift
the stone out of the boat and on to the swaying float, then
over the catwalk, over the granite, to the shore. The two
men are silent. Noting that our wooden wheelbarrow will
make for a very tough uphill climb with our unusual load,
our neighbor Norma Stanley has miraculously appeared
with the four-wheeler and its small trailer. She hauls the
stone to the house, and we place it on the front deck. It
doesn't seem odd to have a gravestone sitting on the deck
in the still bright late afternoon sun. We have time before
the stone must be moved, this time in the wheelbarrow,
down the hill again to the cemetery. There is still time for
the father and remaining son to mark out and prepare the
small grave that will be Ben's place.

The Cuban artist Ana Mendieta, who died at the tragically
young age of 37 in 1985, created in her *Silueta* series of
photographs, "silhouettes" of her own body pressed into,
or superimposed upon, the land. In physical form and in
remarkable images Mendieta accomplishes a powerful
statement about our connection with land and with place.
She transforms an ostensibly empty beach, a border, with
a "silhouette," itself a signifier of absence. Now, years later,
I think we were doing something like that on the day we
arrived at the island with the stone for Ben's grave. With

that arrival, we were about to mark the land, to create a presence out of absence. We were leaving, not the "thing itself," but a trace that we could fill in, endow with whatever reality seemed appropriate. And we were leaving that trace, not to shift with wind and tide on a sandy beach, but to endure in hard ground and rock.

Seekers

Some of us arrive at the dock seeking relaxation and re-spite, some, answers to questions we may not even know we are asking. And still others—protagonists from "away," transients, visitors searching out "information"—may step on to the shore of the island with the wrong question. In any case, it's the asking that counts, that sets the seeker on his or her way. Asking generates the narrative that may reveal its own peculiar truth, especially to those who come, decades later, with quests of their own.

Frankfort, the protagonist in Sarah Orne Jewett's "King of Folly Island," is a visitor with a quest. He seeks sublime landscapes: "dark forest and bleak rocks that seem to have been broken into fragments by some convulsion of nature, and scattered in islands and reefs along the coast." We never learn exactly what Frankfort's questions might entail, what it is that he seeks beyond balm for his own city-worn sensibilities. The ordinary life of a typical island fishing community, replete with the large-scale disorder of its working waterfront, makes him feel "as if he had taken a step backward into an earlier age." But seemingly it's not early enough. Frankfort seeks a stark, pared down human drama; he renounces the ordinary village to find his story on the most isolated island, one that is the furthest out.

Perhaps Gotts Island's most well-known questioner was Katherine Crosby, a writer for the *Boston Globe* who came on in the summer of 1926. Crosby thought she knew what she wanted: to "get the story" of Miss Elizabeth Peterson, who had died the preceding winter in the fire that destroyed her house at the far eastern tip of the island. Unlike Jewett's Frankfort, this visitor from another place comes to the island to find a story that she believes is already there. But she too seeks outer bounds: she has come, she says, to the "edge of nowhere," to find an explanation for an "end that came one stormy night."

With a firm mission and a precise destination, Crosby has come to cover the "Mystery of Gotts Island" and the demise of the "little old lady nearing 70" who lived on its outer edge. As investigative reporter and storyteller, Crosby had already written about Cape Cod's "golden age of romance and adventure," the seventy years between the clipper ships and the automobile; she had interviewed the last of the great captains of sail who were still living in the 1920s. She is clearly drawn to past histories, to disappearing cultures, and to the mysteries enshrouded in them. Here, on Gotts Island, is a story worthy of her investigative talents.

Like myself years later, Crosby is puzzled by Miss Peterson's decision to eschew the village that hugged the quieter, western shore of the island and to build her house on the rocks by the open sea. Her explanation, that Miss Peterson simply followed the instincts of her "Norse Viking stock," seems inadequate at best, a rather obvious imitation of Jewett's description of the strange "King" George Quint, in "The King of Folly Island," who displayed "an uncommon independence" behooving one who came of "old Viking" lineage. "She did love the sea!" Crosby enthuses about Miss Peterson; "and if she couldn't be a sailor she could at least live close to it and share its varying moods. In the winter its spray would splash against her windows when the tide ran high and a southerly storm was blowing."

Yet, despite a predilection for gothic description—this is, after all, a mystery story—Crosby describes a real place.

She lands at Gotts Island in the place where we ourselves have so often arrived: "We landed in a small cove made by a hook of shingly beach," she says, and "went up the main street, which was still part of a field but could be seen by careful observation" to lead up to the houses. The "cove" is the pool, the hook-like bar still its determining feature.

But Crosby wants to move quickly, perhaps too quickly, from the shore. In her haste to get up the path to the village to interview the local inhabitants, she seems not to realize fully that she has come to a foreign place, and the life (and death) she has come to investigate will not be readily fathomable to mainland visitors. The writer is an outsider. She finds the islanders "a fine intelligent lot whose stock has by no means run out in quality," but she is not successful in eliciting the information she seeks. She must press on, further into the interior of the island and ultimately to its far eastern point:

> We followed [Miss Peterson's] trail out through the woods, [through] blue spruce and green, with grassy spaces and banks of wild roses and sweet fern, with air aromatic in the sunshine; [through] the shadow of the denser woods, with gray Spanish moss draped from the branches of the elder trees; out close to shore, with pale pink edges sloping to the sea. [Then, suddenly, we came] upon a clump of flaming poppies; then more flowers—a wealth of them.

We move here from gothic to romance. The island is a place of lush opulence, wild roses and sweet fern, aromatic air. We experience with the reporter both dense shadowy woods and the bright flame of poppies. This is not a setting for gothic mystery or emptiness. The discovery, when it suddenly comes, jars in its stark contrast: among the bright blooms, Crosby sees, more startling than the beauty of the flowers, "some stones outlining the foundation of a house, and the stump of a chimney."

The mystery stands as exactly that. Miss Peterson, the "Norse Viking" descendant who actually came from a well-placed Philadelphia family, remains one of the "strange isolated beings." The investigative reporter has not found her answer. No one has an answer: "Evenings [the islanders] talk it over and over, and over; but by putting everything together that everyone knows or thinks or guesses, they are still no nearer to knowing."

The story that began at the dock ends, abruptly, at the outermost edge of the island. It's a newspaper story, brief and succinct. It's a quest story, its trajectory clear. But something happens along the way, and the journey turns ultimately fruitless. Crosby's story is one of not-knowing; and whether she realized it or not, that makes it a quintessentially island tale.

Ted Is Here

Ted Holmes, who lives just down the hill from us, was born in 1910 and has been coming to Gotts Island since childhood. His wife, Jane, with whom he famously wintered at the island decades ago, died in 1983, and in recent years, with increasing age, Ted's visits to the island have been sporadic. But if there is a hierarchy of summer people organized around the number of years each has been associated with the island, then Ted has claim to seniority. It seemed that Ted and Jane had always been there; they were at the center of all negotiations between the summer and local folks; they knew the lore; and since they lived year round not far away—Ted taught English at the University of Maine in Orono—they seemed to us, the later arrivals, like living avatars of the island's past.

That's why it saddened me to learn on a bright midsummer day that no one, outside of his immediate family, knew that Ted was due to arrive. This was information that I should have learned at the dock.

It was different in the "old days" (for me that means 1960s/1970s) when Russie Gott knew all the arrivals and departures. He knew because he supplied the transportation, using either his old lobster boat, the Margaret Caroline, or the smaller skiff with the outboard. Those were the days when Russie, also known as Rut, brought both the mail and grocery orders every day from HG Reed's store in Bass Harbor.

With the mailbag, with the groceries, with arriving guests or regular island summer people, Russie brought news. News came in various forms: a scratched note on the back of an envelope, a verbal report of a phone call, perhaps even a formal postcard or letter. Whatever the form, news to islanders, especially in the days before phone contact, was manna. Both literally and figuratively, Rut was our lifeline to the mainland. His was the most important arrival of any day.

All the islanders, or at least a representative from each house, waited for Rut. He was supposed to leave Bass Harbor by 12 noon according to the terms of his contract with the U.S. Mail service. With good luck, when the tide was high and he could get into the inner pool, Rut might arrive by, say, 12:30. But that was pretty optimistic. For whatever the weather or tide, Russie never ran the engine of the Margaret Caroline at full throttle. Never.

So it would get to be 1 p.m., and if it happened to be low tide, it would get later than that. Meanwhile the small group of islanders waiting by the "post office"—at one time an old metal Sears Roebuck temporary garden structure that had to be deconstructed in the winter lest it blow away—grew larger. So too the speculation. For no one ever knew which way Russie Gott would arrive on any particular day. We might hear the engine of the Margaret Caroline, then strain to try to see the boat itself appearing out in the channel. On a foggy day there would be sound only, heightening the mystery of the daily drama. Only at a constantly varying point would it be clear which mode of arrival Rut would elect, which way the boat would be heading.

It was all about the tides and Rut's reading of whether he could get over the bar between Big and Little Gotts islands; whether, if he couldn't get over the bar because the tide was too low, he would round Little Gotts and come

in by way of the foreharbor; or whether—and this everyone dreaded—because of weather of some other condition
known only to him, he would moor the Margaret Caroline
"behind the back of the beach," or at the Green Head, and
carry all the groceries and the mail over the Gotts Island
bar, wading across the inner pool, and finally arriving with
the load at the post office.

"Seems like it's always low tide at Gotts Island," Rut would
mutter as he completed the terrible task. Watching for him,
looking forward to the loaf of bread or new jar of peanut
butter that meant we could finally have lunch, that's the
way it seemed to us too.

Russie Gott was a small, grizzled man with wire-framed
glasses, a cap, and high boots. In his drinking days, he sport-
ed a big tummy, but after about 1976, and the famous occasion when he fell off the Margaret Caroline into the pool
at high tide, the drinking ended and the tummy diminished
considerably. It's pretty much gone in the photograph we
have of Russie and Ben together on the Margaret Caroline
the summer when Ben was Russie's diligent, and devoted,
helper. Ben, at eleven, is as tall as Rut. The two seem to be
looking at each other, on the same wave length, the braces
on Ben's teeth plainly in view.

But whatever the circumstance, Russie always took his
responsibilities seriously. Ben—and others—could help
carry the groceries, the "oardahs" as Rut called them; but
no one, absolutely no one, could touch the large canvas bag
with "U.S. Mail" stamped in faded gray letters.

And no one, absolutely no one, could enter the post office—or mail shack—while Russie was sorting the mail.

Protecting our now warm milk, bread, eggs, and once frozen vegetables from the ravages of the sun and peeing dogs, we stood without, expectant, awaiting the news that Russie brought. We chatted and gossiped, sharing our news as we awaited the precious mail. Those receiving letters that day would read them as they stood—sometimes aloud to the group—as if loath to leave the little congregation spread out on the grass outside the shack.

In those years when few people owned a boat of their own, trips to the mainland were occasions, and cell phones nonexistent, that's where we learned who was coming, who going. There would be no surprises. We didn't have to learn, suddenly, that "Ted is here." We knew who was expected. We knew who had arrived.

Grace

I certainly noticed the two large women on the dock but I didn't recognize either of them. Not at first. It was high tide, and I was taking my swim in the pool behind Lyle and Vee Reed's old cottage.

Lyle died in 1991, Vee in 1992, and since their deaths the cottage, or "camp," is now pretty much abandoned. I had the pool to myself today. I tell myself that in this spot the sun heats the rocks and sand of the pool bottom when it is dry at low tide, and this natural heating system makes high tide immersions bearable. But I don't know if that is really true. The real advantage of swimming behind Lyle and Vee's old house is the view of the dock, of who's coming, who's going. If you know what's happening at the dock, you know a lot about Gotts Island. Vee, it was said, used binoculars to track details of activity at the dock, which she could see easily from her house. I just use my eyes, bobbing up like a seal from the water and looking about me.

The two women who had just arrived struggled out of Lyford's small boat, huffing and puffing a bit as they hauled gear up the walkway over the rocks. It wasn't easy even for a slim, fit person. These two women were neither, but their eagerness to get the job done was clearly apparent.

Now a little group was forming and chatting by Mont's old house immediately adjacent to the dock. Uncle Mont, literally a hermit in the winter months in the years preceding his death, was Montell Gott who was born on the island and lived a good part of his life there except for those years when he ran off with the Irish maid of Miss Leffingwell, a summer resident. There were rumors of progeny from this liaison, but no one really knew what happened to the Irish maid, and then Miss Leffingwell sold her large three-story log house to the Strausses.

When the *New York Times* ran an article in the Travel Section about Gotts Island and printed a picture of Uncle Mont's old house, they didn't identify it at all. No, the *Times* simply called the house picturesque, the island an "unfound treasure." They didn't mention that Uncle Mont's old house is strategically located right by the dock and how important that is.

Well, I thought, these two women whom I think I do not know have somehow found the treasure. By this time I had come out of the icy water—my theory of the natural warming does not always hold true—toweled off some of the chill, put on my glasses, and prepared myself for the walk back up the hill to my house.

That's when I realized that I did know one of the new arrivals. It was Grace, much changed in the years since I had seen her, but certainly the same Grace who had rented our house for several summers about twenty years before. She was a painter then and had worked in the upstairs bedroom that was my own favorite place in the house. I loved the painting she did of the fields and ocean refracted through the old glass of the window in that room. How wonderfully she had caught the splendid unevenness of it all.

Grace sent me a photograph of the painting, and I sent her an awkward attempt at a poem about the blue floor in that room that meant so much to us both. We both loved the marine blue on the wide barn boards. And I was touched when Grace and her kids left small natural treasures in the house. Renters often leave pretty rocks, small shells, and the like; but Grace's gifts had been more than that. And her painting of the blue bedroom, with just a hint of the blue ocean beyond the white curtains, with all the imperfections of that room—her painting, even if it didn't belong to me, felt like a gift too.

But that was a long time ago, when Grace was married to the very handsome Bob, who was working back in Portland and didn't come to the island much. She spent much of her time on the island with Russie Gott, who was then approaching seventy and had decided opinions about who was a Gotts Island person and who was not. Grace received the highest marks from Russie—"the best kind of person," he always said. Bob was not mentioned. We didn't know him very well, and when I later heard that Grace and Bob had split up, I had no difficulty at all imagining Grace, raising her kids on her own, and of course, still painting irregularities that showed the wonderful pattern of things.

But the funeral service for Russie was a puzzle. Russie Gott died in June 1991, and when, in early July, the local Masonic order orchestrated the burial of his ashes in the Gotts Island cemetery, Bob was there and Grace wasn't. Not only that: accompanying Bob was a rather glamorous blonde woman whom Russie would certainly have labeled "not an island person." We were all politely standing in the cemetery on that gloomy morning listening to the Masons, who wore little aprons and carried a small spruce tree—"coals to Newcastle," a number of us, unaccustomed to Masonic ritual, were thinking—and remembering the man who had been such an important part of all our island lives, and certainly of Grace's too, even though Grace herself wasn't there.

We had gathered ourselves stiffly in the easternmost part of the cemetery near where Russie's parents, Blanche and Berle, are buried; a place where, according to Northwood, who made the arrangements, Russie had been told in his last awful days of dying with cancer, there was room only for an urn of ashes and not "full coffin" (as they say). Russie wasn't too keen on cremation, Northwood said, but because he really wanted to be buried in that northeast section, near Blanche and Berle, he had agreed to it. So we were burying Russie's ashes, not a coffin, the day when the aproned Masons stood with their little tree to offer their farewell, the day when Bob and the blonde woman stood near the edge of the group and everyone wondered why they were there.

It was about three years after Russie's funeral that I saw Grace and her companion arriving at the dock. They had come, it turned out, to rent the Beamans' house on the extreme north side of the island, looking out to the Bass Harbor lighthouse and the campground and mountains of Acadia. I knew the house well. In the years when the Beamans came regularly themselves, John and I had gone out for dinner many times, following a long, rutted-out track and then turning off at the sign of the blue cat to follow an even more obscure path to the house on its low bluff overlooking the sea. Dick Beaman was an abstract expressionist painter with a particularly wry wit. It was easy to understand why, in the days when he was still teaching both studio and history of art, the lecture hall was packed when he gave his Dada lecture. The sign with the blue cat was typical of his view of the world: just beneath the cat itself with its glaring yellow eyes, an inscription announced, "We're all crazy here."

The way to the Beamans' house was not easy by day and almost impossible at night. Visitors navigated their way among blown down trees, a thicket of raspberry bushes, and marshy spots only barely covered by pieces of drift-wood. No wonder that at a certain age Dick acquired a four-wheeler to haul his groceries out there—and himself until he got too stiff to throw his leg up and over the seat.

But I was not thinking of the cat, or of the difficult path, on that bright day in July when I learned that Grace and her friend were planning to walk with their gear out to the Beamans' house. The friend, I was told, would be leaving the next day, and Grace could have a week on her own in that beautiful and remote place. As a painter, she would surely love being there, I thought. The view from the deck is magnificent, a kind of counterpoint to Dick's 3'x5' abstract painting of green tides and trees that has hung for years on the living room wall. Dick had done the painting outside and just incorporated the gull droppings and spruce sap in the work.

I looked forward to seeing Grace during her stay. She would have to come along the town road at some point—everyone does—and I would intercept her and invite her to come up to the house and tell me the news about her new life as an illustrator, about her now-grown kids, and so on. Catching up after so many years would be a special pleasure.

But the days went by and I saw no sign of Grace. Even without binoculars, I can see from that upstairs bedroom window, in the room where she had painted, everyone who comes along the road. I kept thinking I would see her. But I didn't.

"That's because she isn't here," Carl, a close neighbor and friend, said.

We were sitting around the heavy pine farmer's table in our kitchen, under the old hanging kerosene light that always made black rings on the ceiling when the wick was turned too high. Carl had delivered surprising news. But I trust his information. He has a good boat, as well as a rowing shell, and he spends time around the dock. He knows what's happening.

Grace got appendicitis in the middle of the night, Carl reported. She had walked over to his house and asked him to take her off the island to the hospital. And he did.

"Appendicitis?"

This couldn't be true. Years ago in New Jersey, I'd had an appendix attack and in the one-mile drive to the hospital, where I was to remain for ten days, I had experienced the most excruciating pain I had ever felt. It was searing, gut-ripping pain. No one with appendicitis could have walked in the middle of the night down the Beamans' primitive path. How was this possible?

I wanted to get to the bottom of this. I pressed on, thinking of the agony that Grace must have felt on that path while the rest of us slept on in the dark Gotts Island night. I pushed Carl for more detail.

He suddenly looked sheepish.

"Well, that's not really how it happened," he said. "Grace didn't have an appendicitis attack. She came to my door, and said she wanted to die. That's why she had to get to the hospital. I saw that the situation was serious, and it was high tide. So I took her off in my boat and then drove her over to the hospital in Bar Harbor."

I had an answer, but not the one I was expecting.

Later I would wonder why I pressed on that way. But perhaps I had learned something too, something about distance, about suffering that comes of distance and ignorance. The end of the story didn't match the beginning. The scene at the dock was out of joint. Grace had arrived on the dock that day no doubt with an expectation of what her island stay would be. She must have looked forward to coming back to the island after so many years. But then she had suffered in the Beamans' lovely but remote house by the sea, at the end of the path marked by the sign of the crazy cat. And none of us had known. We were one small island, and we had not known.

Renewal

The chairs arrived at the dock on the day before the wedding. They came on Lyford's boat along with the champagne, the glasses, and the tent. We have a photograph of the entire wedding party, plus numerous friends and family, arranged on the shore just in front of the dock, all dressed for the work of carrying the chairs from the dock, over the rocks, to Northwood Kenway's jeep for the trip up to the house. We're all feeling the heat of an unusually warm day, but we look happy, preparing for the celebration to come.

Another photograph was taken the next day, another arrival at the dock. It's the day of the wedding. With the chairs now arranged in place at the house, this photograph captures the arrival of Chris's bride, Kathy, her family, and the first contingent of wedding guests. Kathy holds aloft her simple 1920s style wedding dress of floating silk, and steps daintily in small gold sandals on to the rough boards. Chris, in a white linen suit modeled on the one worn by Humphrey Bogart when he married Lauren Bacall, welcomes his bride to the island. He wears a straw boater and wing-tip shoes. They are of the past but not in the past.

They are a couple who ten months earlier waltzed on the rocks in the rain where the pool meets the sea. They are dressed like summer islanders from another era in this photograph that goes out with the wedding announcement. The photo, slightly murky, seems to have spent years pasted to a page of an old album. Its message designates the wedding date, which, unbeknownst to the future guests, has been chosen because high water comes at noon on that day. Ultimately 110 people plan their vacations in order to be on Gotts Island on July 15 of the next summer for this wedding.

Through the months of winter and spring, the wedding plans progress. My nephews, who run a summer cruise business in Bass Harbor, will transport the guests to the island and back in their boats. It will take three trips. Tide charts are consulted once again. Since we can get the boats in to the dock about two hours before and two hours after the high tide, we have a window of four hours. Kathy sends the schedule of boat departures out with the formal invitation that she has designed.

But the real design is in the chairs. It's Kathy who insists that we collect as many chairs as we can from the neighbors and import eighty more out to the island so that all the guests can sit down. All the occasions I remembered at Gotts Island had been stand-up affairs. We stood in the cemetery to remember Ben's life on the island as we buried his ashes; we stood for Russie Gott's memorial as well. But now we will sit. A great-nephew, age fourteen, is enlisted to gather up the chairs. So they come together: the summer house tubular aluminum chairs with torn tapes, the one-arm-loose or spoke-missing farmhouse oak chairs from our own attic, the benches from the Kenways' picnic table, a motley assemblage from garden, attic, and shed that contrasts with the orderly rented imports.

Chris wants the chairs set up on the north side of the house, and weeks before any of us have arrived on the island, a neighbor has mowed that field, cutting out every trace of elder root or juniper. It's as smooth as hummocky smooth can be at Gotts Island. Three days before the wedding, John and I pace off the space, consider the angle of the sun, and mark where the chairs will be. With unusual precision, John uses string to mark out "aisles" to guide the young chair movers.

It makes no difference that brief but heavy showers the morning of the wedding alter the plan. Every seat acquires a small puddle, every towel and cloth in the house is pressed into service, all the chairs are moved to the south side and the protection of the tent—in rows that will be considerably less orderly. No matter. We will sit to celebrate this wedding.

The guests who arrived on the dock on the wedding day came with the usual expectations of island visitors. They were ready to learn the cues in a prescribed route from the dock that John had marked with stakes topped with carefully arranged bunches of flowers. They would pass, just as Katherine Crosby had done, the white fence of the cemetery. But unlike the writer of seventy years before, they would see, in the far northwest quadrant, the huge bouquet of blue delphinium that John, Chris, and I had placed on Ben's grave that morning. They would know from the start that Ben was included, that the island, and this celebration, could accommodate both loss and joy.

It was the chairs that told so much of the story. By the time the tide had turned, the pool was emptying, and the guests had departed, the chairs, once so orderly arranged, sat in disheveled silence. The fancy imports would be packed off from the dock the next day, the broken borrowings returned. But for the moment, all remained, still bearing the traces of the happiness of the occasion, an acknowledgment that the fragility of life need not negate our commitment to the future.

3

BOARDING

"I remember when we boarded with the Moores," Ted Holmes used to say, usually as preamble to a Gotts Island reminiscence. He was referring to the 1920s and the years when he, a summer visitor from New Jersey, first came to know the Moore family. "The room I stayed in was a front room, a small bedroom, and I could look out at the pool," another ex-boarder remarked.

It was always known, at least from about 1900, as the "Moore house"; but for me, it is almost as important that the house was a boarding house. Summer people all, the boarders knew the coherent year-round community that ultimately disintegrated. They were not of the community, but they lived, at least for short periods, with it. And since a number of the boarders ultimately purchased the island property left by the old residents, they became the new summer community: a community not of boarders but of vacation homeowners. Most of the Moores' boarders are gone themselves now, but their generation intersected with my own. They told and retold the old stories, in various and sundry versions, to the younger summer families. They were the mediators between us, the present summer people, and "them," the year-round islanders of the past.

The boarders in the Moore house belonged in something of the same way that we now belong. We have the worries and the responsibilities, as well as the joys and security, of own-ership; but like the old boarders at the house, we come, we go, and then we come back again.

And all the while, albeit empty of people now in fall, win-ter, and spring, the house stays. Hundreds of miles away from us, it belongs to itself. But we know it is there. In the decades that we have owned the Gotts Island house we lived abroad three times, moved three times, and for sixteen years maintained a bi-coastal marriage with homes in New Jersey and California. When asked about the latter arrangement—as we often were—the answer was always the same: "But we are always together at Gotts Island in the summer."

The island house is an anchor in our lives, a steady point that sustains us through all our moves, physical and emo-tional. It is property, and much more than property. Look-ing out to the cemetery and the sea beyond, firmly rooted in the village of which it is a part, the house situates us, just as it did its earlier occupants, in the life of the island. It is large, sprawling, capacious. It accommodates generations of us all. It is a fixed center, a site of memory and imagina-tion. And at the same time, in witnessing the coming and going—and coming again—of boarders, it is an acknowl-edgment of the transience of life itself.

Coming Back

The return to the house is always the same. I haul up my hand baggage while Norma Stanley brings up the books, luggage, and groceries in the trailer behind the four-wheeler. I could ride with Norma, but I want to walk, to trudge up the path, past where the alders grew until last summer when they were, once again, cut down. I want to approach slowly, to climb up the hill and see the roof line, three white triangles, and finally the entire structure of our house rise gradually to view.

The hill is really two slopes, separated by the relatively flat field that situates the cemetery. Russie Gott, born on Gotts Island in 1910, used to say that when the island kids ran their sleds down from the very top of the hill, they always slowed to a halt right by the cemetery where the ground leveled out. Only on a very cold winter day, when the path was especially icy, could they keep their sleds going, all the way down to the pool. I think of that frigid dusk, the shivering sledders, anxious to leave the precinct of the cemetery as the winter darkness came on.

But I have never seen that winter. Now, in the bright summer sun, I reach the top of the first slope, where the old town road, a broadened track, crosses the path. All five original village houses are before me now, all five preserved or rehabilitated by summer people. My own house is in full view, at the top of the second slope. This is the village of the living. At its center, just to the left of where I am now standing, is the island cemetery, the enclosure of the dead that Russie and his generation of island children had tried to avoid.

The two entrances to the cemetery, both on the east side and always open—their intricately carved gates long since gone and never replaced—remain as simple blanks in the fence, wide enough to accommodate a horse and wagon, broad enough to suggest that the worlds of the living and the dead may not be so separate after all.

Bridging the gap between the living and dead is the work of the living who seek to understand the meaning of those they have lost. I'm standing now in the exact spot that was the destination of Ruth Moore's fictionalized character Phebe Bunker when she returned to Gotts Island from the world of the dead. Moore tells this story in a poem called "The Ghost of Phebe Bunker," but she would have known a real Phebe—one Phebe Gott. This Phebe was the daughter of Erastus and the sister of Berlin and Montell, who both lived to old age, and of Martin and Paris who drowned to-gether at the ages of 21 and 15 respectively; she was the mother of Austin, whose father was never identified and whom I knew only slightly as the very handsome man who in the early 1970s drowned in the waters off Black Island en route to an ill-fated romantic tryst.

Phebe in the poem came back to the island and the remains of a house that Ruth Moore—and I—know well. She too climbed the hill but saw, not cut fields and cleanly painted white houses but, rather, "roofless, windowless houses / An alder-grown curved road climbing a hill, / A wilderness wilder than it started out to be." Phebe returned to an is-land of the disappeared; the timbered roofs and walls hav-ing long since fallen, only the foundation stones remained to mark the people who had once lived there. Everything was lost to the ever encroaching spruce and alder.

Only in memory could Phebe envision her house—my house—"standing, plain as could be." But standing at the entrance to the cemetery today, I can see it clearly, the house Ruth Moore would have imagined when she wrote the poem. It's still there, now with replaced sills, walls, and roof. It's still linked, both visually and symbolically, to the stones in the island cemetery.

Phebe came back to the stone marked with her own name. I am on my way to the small granite stone that marks Ben's grave. Unobtrusive and flat against the ground, Ben's stone makes no attempt to compete with the tall, much more elaborate, nineteenth-century stones that are its neighbors here. But it draws us like a magnet. It's always the first stop when John and I return to the island. I put my bags down in the blank space where the southernmost gate once stood. I traverse the geography I know so well. I too have a destination.

It's almost a year since I have seen the stone. I need to know how it has weathered the winter, if it looks the same as last year. By late June, Northwood will have scrupulously cut the grasses and trimmed the weeds in the island cemetery. Nothing obstructs the flat stone, the simple lettering that announces the death of a young man, age twenty-six, killed in an accident in East Africa.

"Hello, Ben. We're back."

The greeting is the same as it was last year and the years before that. Its words echo Ben's own as a teenager, when he would return, too often late, on a Saturday night and knock softly on our bedroom door: "Hi. I'm back."

In the text of his Nobel acceptance speech the Japanese writer Kenzaburo Oe speaks of the boy in *The Adventures of Nils* who understands the language of birds and undertakes an adventurous journey to roam with wild geese. The future novelist first read the story as a child, when he was sent out to a remote island in the Japanese Archipelago to escape the ravages of World War II. Oe the child loved the story. Oe the adult loves the memory of reading it on the distant island. It was, he says, a story of return. The boy decides to come back to his parents: "Mother, Father," he says, "I'm a human being again!"

Phebe came back. Nils, the boy in Kenzaburo Oe's story, came back. These are wondrous returns; but they are beyond the experience of most of us. We must find our consolations without the aid of miracles. I leave Ben's stone, pick up the baggage I have left by the cemetery entrance, and begin the final climb up to the house. There the usual opening up chores await us. There's a pump and water system to be reinstalled, screen doors must be put up, floors swept, rooms aired, shelves scrubbed down, beds made up. At least for now there will be little time to stand on the front deck and look back down the hill toward the cemetery and the sea beyond.

But I am back, and the small flat piece of granite marked with Ben's name is just as I left it the preceding summer. The center still holds. I look up once again toward the hill and the house. There it sits, at the highest point of the island, its broad vista sweeping out to the western sea and sky. Still firmly anchored.

Belongings

No, the island does not belong only to itself; and the house and its contents belong only in a narrow sense to us. But it's not ultimately a matter of who owns what. It's about whose presence is there. How do we live with these other inhabitants, the spaces they have occupied, the objects they have left behind?

Ruth Moore is one of several presences to be reckoned with. "I read Ruth Moore," announced the bumper sticker on a Maine car I saw in Bass Harbor last summer. The message was not so surprising. In the 1990s Ruth's books were republished in paperback by a local Maine press and now join the ever-lengthening shelf of local literature produced in part for an expanding tourist market. Place makes literature; literature makes place. On the back cover of Ruth's published letters appears a wonderful old photograph of the island cemetery with our house rising up behind it. The photograph, taken no doubt when Ruth was the owner, seems to announce that the house will always be hers.

Articles in *Down East* magazine and in the Travel Section of the *New York Times* tell a similar story, the latter even providing directions to the house (follow the town road, turn right at the path, and so on). Of course, not surprisingly, no one ever appeared at our door, *Times* in hand, asking for a tour of Ruth Moore's house. And this was a relief. We do not want our islands, the places where we dwell, to belong to the world; we fear the loss of our own imaginative grasp. Perhaps that's why Ruth wrote, I think disingenuously, that "the offshore islands belong to themselves." She needed to keep the world at bay in order to shape her own version of Gotts Island, the version that would truly belong to her.

How can we shape a house and its contents—its "marks," images, and yes, objects—such that they will lend credibility and pattern to our own lives? Where, among the traces, do we ourselves belong?

It's almost faded into oblivion now: "Hannah, her mark," the grayed writing on the deed says. And then comes the wavering "x." She was Hannah Norwood Gott, wife of Daniel Gott, who purchased what became Gotts Island for £18 in 1789. Her mark appears on the original deed to the property that was transferred to John and me in 1965. The deed, now framed, occupies its own particular spot on the living room wall.

In 1812, with that deed, Daniel and Hannah passed property on to one of their twelve children (the Gotts were "a vigorous hearty race," says Dr. H. W. Small in his History of Swan's Island, Maine, published in 1898). Some of the twelve moved away to other islands and to towns on the mainland. Nathaniel, one of those who stayed, became the father of Asenath, who married the first Philip Moore, grandfather of Ruth Moore's father, another Philip. Two other sons of Daniel and Hannah drowned with their father on a June day in 1814 when bad weather overtook them as they fished in a whale boat near Mount Desert Rock. This would have been two years after Hannah inscribed her mark.

Perhaps if Hannah had actually written her own name I would be able to see her more clearly as a person. But oddly, the more enigmatic "Her mark" has a permanence—despite the graying ink—that transcends an individual life. It is an artifice of existence as opposed to existence itself.

A place of loss, a place of life

Ghosts gather round the pine farm table between the wood stove and the windows

Further along the wall, where the living room flows into the front hall, is the 1902 official document wherein the Postmaster General of the United States appoints Ruth Moore's father, the second Philip, as official postmaster of Gotts Island. Between the property deed and the postal certificate lie the long, interrelated histories of the Moores and the Gotts. Postmaster Philip and his wife Lovina (Vinie) acquired the house in 1901, and with it took over the store and the post office that had been the domain of its earlier owner, Andrew J. Gott. Vinie began to take in summer boarders, and ultimately she and Philip raised a family of three girls and one boy. By 1930, when all the year-round inhabitants were leaving, Philip and Vinie, like their neighbors, had left the house; and in the way of those who left other islands in Maine, they left the contents too.

It was only many years later that more objects, items belonging to us, arrived. In 2004, on a gray day threatening rain, I stood on the dock in Bass Harbor, and with expectation of disaster watched a chest of drawers, a pine dining table, a smaller side table, and six boxes, some fragile, pass by in Lyford's small outboard powered skiff.

"I thought he was using the big boat for this load," I mumbled fearfully to John. But no, there in Lyford's small boat were belongings from our recently sold New Jersey house en route to becoming Gotts Island belongings.

The occasion, luckily not marked by catastrophe, was nonetheless momentous. It was the first time in almost forty years that we had moved objects that belonged to us into the Gotts Island house. Each summer we would arrive with our clothes, books, and papers; and each summer we took all of this away when we returned to New Jersey.

The only items I left were strictly practical: sheets, towels, small kitchen utensils.

The real contents of the house remained, seemingly with a life of their own. The old wicker chairs, worn chests of drawers, beds with sagging mattresses were all in the house when we bought it from my sister in 1965; and much of it was there when she bought the place from Ruth Moore in 1958. The bed in the best guest room is now fitted out with an improved mattress and figures hand painted by John on its head and foot boards, but it still has a long history in the house. The organ was moved well before our time from its special room on the far side of the living room into its present spot in the kitchen. It no doubt played a central role when the Moores, their friends, and perhaps the summer boarders too gathered round to sing "I'll Take You Home Again Kathleen."

All of these objects belong, and yet do not belong, to us. In a recent volume of poems titled *Belongings*, Sandra Gilbert provides a moving meditation on the meaning of objects, "belongings," to an elderly woman suffering the onset of dementia and a paranoid belief that the objects of her home will be stolen from her. Through her possessions—the Wedgewood, the silver, the walnut table—the ninety-year-old woman attempts to hold on to her own life, her own memories. Her very being is inscribed within these "belongings." To be faced with leaving them, in a move to a nursing home, is to be paralyzed with fear and anxiety.

We are not invested in this way in the contents of a house, barn, and post office that belong both to us and to lives that have preceded us. Whatever the Gotts Island house and its contents meant to their original owners, who departed and left them to their fate, as if dispossessing them, I know they are not my belongings in the sense that Sandra Gilbert describes. Perhaps this very fact explains my peculiar attachment to them. They belong to something larger, and through them I also belong: to a history, to lives that I do not even know.

As both mnemonics and vessels of memory, the contents of the house, fragments of a past, demand a kind of trust. They are only temporarily mine, more powerful to the degree that they are not in a real sense my "property." In the store and adjacent post office cubicle where islanders once gathered to exchange news and gossip, lies a collection of chipped and cracked crockery, disassembled Aladdin and Rayo lamps whose assorted parts we will never reconfigure, remnants of tools and fishing nets we will never repair, biscuit tins rusted almost beyond recognition, and a postal slot through which no letter or postcard will pass. The old wooden store counter is gouged with wear, and the once whitewashed shelves are more gray than white. But the labeling on those shelves—peas, sugar, baking soda—is still legible; and the small red money drawer under the counter pulls out like magic. I can feel the smooth edges of the rounded cup-like change containers where Philip scooped up the pennies and nickels.

In a loft over the store sits the large canister of coffee that apparently never sold and was still there when the Moores left. I estimate this coffee to be more than eighty years old. It's at least as old as the organ, the kerosene lamps, and the run of *American Mercuries* piled up in the attic of the main house.

"How does the coffee taste?" I'm asked.

"I don't know. Never got that desperate."

We will never drink that coffee, but neither do we throw it out. For how can we destroy something that doesn't really belong to us?

Esther

It was only when Ruth Moore died that anyone seemed to remember the papers belonging to her that had been moldering in the attic for decades. The papers—a few undergraduate essays, a photograph album, even a few letters—had been simply there, exerting a particular presence and seemingly at home in a place of odd objects.

But now a neighbor brought word from the mainland that Esther Moore Trask, Ruth's sister, planned to come out to Gotts Island to collect them for the Maine Women Writers Collection in Portland. As usual with such messages, we didn't know just when Esther would be coming; everything depends on weather and tide. But thus forewarned, we foraged about in the attic and brought down whatever we could find.

The sky was gray with light rain falling on the day that Esther and her son Buddy appeared at our door. Esther, whom I estimated to be in her early eighties, was the youngest of the Moore girls. Buddy, a soft-spoken high school teacher, quietly took a seat beside his mother on my stiff wicker sofa. I offered tea.

Esther spoke of the island, the house, and her own birth in the bedroom over the kitchen where Chris slept when we brought him, as an infant, to the island for the first time. She remembered the years when Vinie took in the summer boarders. I have the post card photo of a small girl, about three or four, standing in front of our house. The card says "Hillside Cottage, Gotts Island, Maine." The little girl, Russie Gott told me the summer he gave me the post card, is Ruth Moore. That dates it about 1906 or 1907. The boarders at Hillside cottage must have been a regular feature of the Moore family life when Esther was born. Perhaps Vinie had to take time away from her stove to retire to the room over the kitchen to bring her second daughter into the world.

I did not ask where Philip, the father and husband, was. I know him only by his handwriting, a spidery scrawl with elegant flourishes that he used to keep the account books of the store. Russie Gott told me that Philip was punctilious to a fault when it came to opening the post office at the appointed moment. I fantasize the store as Philip's precinct, but Esther said otherwise; she said that the girls helped out there too, most of the time in fact. Perhaps he was fishing, perhaps mending the nets in the way Ruth would describe in her novel, *The Weir*. The remains of Philip's weir, a straggling line of rocks traversing the outer pool, are still visible when the tide is especially low between Gotts and Little Gotts Islands. That's where we can find the largest mussels on Gotts Island.

In the album we are giving to Esther are photographs of the Moore girls and their chums at teachers college in the 1920s. The images are sepia gray and grainy, but the faces look out with a kind of playful exuberance. Perhaps the young women are happy to have escaped the confinement of the island. Perhaps not.

They must have been tough, these young women who grew up on an offshore island. I try to imagine their lives. Beyond these fragmented images, I know them through the books they read as youngsters, left behind to be piled—like the album and the papers—willy-nilly in the attic. Summerhouse reading material is a genre of its own: in addition to the 1924 run of *American Mercury*, we have old copies of *Saturday Evening Post*, *Life*, and *National Geographic*; *Lassie* and *My Friend Flicka*, short fiction of Edgar Allen Poe, *The Mayor of Casterbridge* and *Silas Marner*. It's a jumble of books and magazines, summer reading brought by later genera- tions of children and adults mixed up with books that be- longed to the Moore family. I imagine the girls, under the kerosene lamp, reading *Rebel of the School*, the story of a tomboy daughter of a rich Irish gentry family who succeeds in outwitting her classmates and teachers at a posh English girls boarding school. I think of that time and class bound language against the shrieking winds of a Maine winter.

But it's all so long ago. Now, on a summer day in 1990, as Esther tells me the stories from the past, John Clark and Scott Swann are tearing off the clapboard that had wrapped the house for almost 150 years. The grass around the foundation is littered with broken, jagged strips of the old wood. This is the first truly major thing we have done to the house. I am thrilled with the notion that the house is being rewrapped for 100 more years; I fantasize future generations, children and grandchildren. As each new clap- board is cut and adjusted, I stand and admire. Scott lov- ingly caulks the old panes in the bay window. All the other windows will be new, but these are odd-sized, difficult or expensive to replace, and will be kept. Scott sands. And caulks more. And sands. And paints. The neighbors come by to admire and approve. That's what happens when you live in an icon.

All this work and effort meant that we were outwitting Ruth's rendering of the island. Her vision of "roofless, win- dowless houses / An alder-grown curved road climbing a hill/A wilderness wilder than it started out to be" would not come to pass. Not yet. We make our brave attempts to forestall inevitable loss.

Perhaps that's what Esther was doing that day as she sat in my living room and recreated the days of her childhood in that house. She had come, after all, to collect Ruth's papers and memorabilia of both of their childhoods. What purpose in preserving the papers if not to keep alive a past? And what purpose in rebuilding a house if not to keep it and its history, even an imagined history, alive for ourselves and our own children?

Outside the sky grows darker. Buddy quietly reminds us that we have to watch both weather and tide if he and his mother are going to get back to the mainland that afternoon. Esther, drinking her tea slowly, is speaking of the departure of the original villagers: the exodus that spelled the end of the life she and her sisters had known as girls. They had gone like Esther, to return only briefly and as visitors, or like Ruth, to return almost not at all.

Harvey, Esther and Ruth's brother, joined their father in wanting to leave the island, Esther explains. She says that Vinie and the girls didn't want to go. I wonder about that move, that walk down the hill toward the waiting boat. It couldn't have been like modern moving. One wouldn't move from a house and leave behind—as Ruth did—one's high school diploma and freshman composition assignments. Perhaps they didn't see themselves as moving at all. They could and would come back. Ruth's letters to Vinie, written in the 1940s, speak about return. But it didn't really happen.

Buddy is right. The water is draining out of the pool. If they are to catch the tide, they must be on their way. We find plastic bags to wrap around the album and the papers. We put the bundles carefully in the wheelbarrow and bid our visitors good-bye. I watch them walk down the hill with their burden, Esther with straight and steady gait, her son pushing the wheelbarrow before him. In the early approaching dusk, the grasses blow wet in the field. I watch until the two figures disappear around the curve where the rose bushes grow, leaving their imprint in the path.

Esther Moore Trask died in 2002. She may have returned to Gotts Island after that day when we gave her Ruth's papers, but I never saw her again.

The Empress

She stood patiently as we denuded her, removing the heavy iron cooking surfaces, the over door, the remains of the rusted out firebox, separating her body from its solid base. We were preparing the Empress Atlantic for her final trip from Gotts Island.

Patented by the Portland Stove Company in 1898, the old Empress was nearing her end. The supports that held the wood in the firebox had finally collapsed entirely, and we couldn't change the draft from "kindle" to "bake" without causing eruptions of smoke that threatened the newly installed white kitchen ceiling. Life had simply gone from the Empress.

Three weeks earlier, in the precincts of Mr. Bryant's stove shop *cum* museum in Thorndike, Maine, at a crossroads somewhere between Waterville and Bangor, John and I had walked the aisles along which rows of rehabbed wood stoves stood at attention with dowager sedateness. We were witnessing the most amazing collection of wood stoves in the state of Maine, and possibly the whole United States. Here they stood, the straight and solidly angular, the curvaceous and flamboyantly curlycued, all presenting themselves to our admiring eyes.

One wonderfully curved specimen seductively flashed herself before us. I imagined myself poised before her, pot in hand, perhaps preparing some lovely omelet with just a bit of cream and lobster. "Too wide," John announced. "It won't fit in the space between the wood box and the door to the back hall and the store."

Of course he was right. Those lovely curves and arabesques would have to be renounced. We continued our walk through Mr. Bryant's collection. And in the second aisle I made an important discovery: our old Empress had siblings, all produced by the company in Portland at the turn of the twentieth century. The Empress was the plain sister, the quiet, perhaps even virginal, member of a family that included the larger, much more matronly models, the Queen and the Duchess. The Empress, despite her name, presented a spare, angular front quite at odds with the broad, heavily ornamented bosoms of her royal sisters. I felt at home with the Empress in a way I never would with the Queen or the Duchess. We knew the Empress would fit because her identical twin had fit.

"There's no question about it. It has to be the Empress," John said.

He was, once again, right.

But what an Empress she was. We saw before us the vanished youth and beauty of our old stove. The handles of the oven and woodbox door were shiny nickel, matching the simply ornamented trim on the cooking surface. A thermometer graced the front of the oven door, and all the drafts and dampers turned at the lightest pressure. In every detail, this was the stove, rehabbed to former glory, that our old one had once been.

A stove just like this had once come, in another time and another world, to our house on Gotts Island. I imagined Vinie Moore, in 1918, ordering the stove from the salesman who traveled around small Maine towns with the tiny scale models—miniature Empresses, Queens, and Duchesses—that now inhabit, splendidly, the top shelf on one whole wall of Mr. Bryant's shop. I imagined—and this is imagination because I do not know the real history of our old Empress, only that the stove was already old in the 1950s—Vinie, perhaps with her husband, Philip, planning, as we did, which model in the Portland Stove Company's family of stoves would fit by the back door, which would serve her needs when she cooked for her family in the winter, and in the summer for both the family and the vacationing boarders.

And I thought about how may times John and I had stoked up that stove; how many pairs of wet socks and sneakers had been placed beneath it; how many hands had rubbed themselves together over its warmth on a cold foggy day; how many times I had warned visiting children not to touch the stove and certainly not to open the door of the firebox; how many meals we had eaten at the long farmhouse table with the Empress comforting (even roasting) the backs of those sitting on that side of the table.

But she could not last forever, that old Empress. All reigns must come to an end. That's what I was thinking as my neighbors Lyford and Vince, with Herculean strength, swiftly heaved the rusty old lady, with all the assorted fragments and pieces, out toward the waiting trailer. She was on her way down to the boat that would take her to Mr. Bryant and what could be a spectacular renewal.

Speed was essential, for the same high tide on which Lyford and Vince were hauling away the old would bring on the new. At this moment, the heiress apparent was wait-

ing on the dock in Bass Harbor for her trip to the island.
The house would experience not a single change of the tide
without an Empress enthroned between the wood box and
kitchen door.

Multiple Occupancy

The specific designation of rooms within a house is a relatively late historical development, but one that for most of us is now a fact of life. In the normal house, a bedroom is a bedroom. One has a bedroom, which usually remains one's bedroom. There are parents' rooms and children's rooms—though the latter may become the teenager's room, the college student's room, even the young marrieds' room and so on. Rooms dedicated to offspring change definition across the life trajectory, but the distinction between "child's room" and "master bedroom" remains pretty much intact.

Not so the Gotts Island house, a house of many bedrooms. When the Moores took in the boarders, the change in seasons must have meant major changes in the sleeping arrangements. The old story is that Ruth hated the arrival of the summer boarders, hated being evicted from her usual bedroom and forced to sleep in the attic. I imagine the family undergoing their seasonal move within the house, the children hauling their clothes, books, and other personal belongings up to the attic.

When we bought the house in 1965 the Moores' erstwhile front parlor had already been converted into the master bedroom. It opens off the current living room, once, probably, a kitchen/dining room; and we know it was an important room because it still has a bay window looking out to the ocean, fancy molding around the windows, and a place where a parlor stove once entered the chimney. In 1965 it was also the only room with intact ceiling and walls when the plaster in the rest of the house was crumbling over our heads. It was a special room.

This ex-parlor became our bedroom. Chris and Ben, aged then three years and seven months respectively, were ensconced in the adjacent small room that also opened off the living room and had once, long before our time, been enlarged to accommodate the organ. In this room, a bedroom once the organ was moved to the kitchen, the boys were close to hand, close enough that any voice in the dark—and it is very dark indeed in a house with no electricity—could be heard.

"Remember when Ben refused to sleep in the small room and moved upstairs?" Chris, now a father himself, recently remarked. I did not remember, perhaps because such a memory would get in the way of my wanting to think of *a* children's room, a constant at the center of the house.

It's as if I cannot tolerate the thought of Ben's move out of that space. And yet it would have made perfect sense: Ben was always wanting to move to somewhere, to exert his independence. That's why, years later, he went to Africa. Yes, it's quite natural that he would have wanted his own room in another part of the house; but it's also quite natural that I have suppressed that small event.

The house no doubt has always had its separate domains, perhaps especially in those days when Ruth Moore, wearing a white pinafore, appeared on the post card to attract prospective boarders to "Hillside Cottage." Perhaps the boarders had zones too: "Keep out: family space." This seems unlikely, but everyone continues to talk about how angry Ruth was about that summertime move to the attic.

A chart of the house would show that it still has its separate spaces. This is in part a feature of its strange architecture:

it's two houses stuck together, a kitchen wing and a living room/bedroom wing. The bedroom above the kitchen, the room accessible only by its own staircase, was for a time my mother's room. Privacy and escape from children's noise were, for her, worth the intrusion of the occasional wayward bat. Years later, after my mother's death, this room, replastered and painted white to make the best of a stunning view, became the guest room.

The guest room is still a room for grown-ups. As an adult, Ben occupied it with his friend Michelle on his last visit to Gotts Island. I remember that the room was still under construction that summer. He and Michelle had to negotiate the staircase up from the back hall with great care, crawl over planks left by the carpenters, watch out for plasterboard and dust. A few years later, Chris and Kathy, before they were parents, took over the now transformed space.

When Peter, Chris and Kathy's first child, arrived on the scene, the house had to be reconfigured once again. Peter came first to Gotts Island when he was eighteen months old. John and I borrowed a fifty-two-year-old crib from my sister, set it up in the old children's room downstairs, and moved upstairs ourselves, leaving the parlor/master bedroom to the young parents. At least temporarily, I got a "new" room, one I had never slept in, the small white room trimmed in Scandinavian blue on the east side. John took the yellow one next to it. Another year, with another family visit, we might reverse that. As grandparents, John and I move upstairs to leave the family accommodation to the younger generation. Ben and Chris's room became Peter's room, and still later, Peter and his sister Astrid's room.

We don't feel displaced; it's just that parents should sleep in the room adjacent to where the young children are. And children should not be at the top of steep stairs. We occupy the house according to where we are in our lives. Sometimes I have afternoon light in my bedroom, sometimes morning light. Sometimes I look out to the ocean, sometimes the back field and the woods. We are flexible; the house is flexible.

This may simply mean that the house can be viewed, and used, in a number of ways. Or it may mean that we are all boarders here. We board in the places that are most central to our lives. Where our relationship seems most sporadic or tenuous it is actually the most secure. We do not simply dwell in the islanded summer house. We also imagine. We dream.

4

GATHERING

The Perfect Medium

In a 1960 book titled *Ghost Towns of New England* Gotts Island is listed as a bona fide ghost town. This may mean that the village, or my own house, *is* a ghost—that is, a vestige—of an earlier existence that has left its objects to us; but more exactly, the island is a place where ghosts gather. They are here, waiting for us, the living, to reanimate them in story and in memory.

Mechanical trickery was behind the photographs of ghosts featured in a recent Metropolitan Museum exhibit called "The Perfect Medium." Like the ghosts on display, images in memory, voices from the past, may also call for a suspension of our rational capacities. For they never completely disappear, these ghosts. Morphing into ever more opaque beings, they leave their traces—a garment, a letter, fragments of language. Some, the more familiar, lie close to the surface of memory and experience; others are more deeply buried, surprising us with their intensity when we come upon them.

As I sit in the old wicker chair in the corner of the kitchen, I can almost hear their voices. They are the ghosts who gather around the big pine farm table between the wood stove and the windows. They are the people who have been part of that room over the forty years we have lived in the house. They were the visitors: my large family of aunts, uncles, and cousins who played cards at the kitchen table by the light of the ever blackening hanging kerosene lamp; friends from graduate school and the early years of John's career, students and colleagues we have known in three universities, neighbors from the various places we have called home in the non-summer months, colleagues from abroad, and on and on.

"Remember the time that Jim [the heavy smoker] arrived on the island and discovered that he had left all his cigarettes back in his car on the mainland?" we might say. Or, "Remember the time that Doug brought a half gallon of gin and several bottles of tonic only to learn that we had no refrigerator on the island and he would have to drink gin and tonic without ice?" Or what about Sam, a graduate student who had never touched a hammer in his life but suddenly found himself down on hands and knees helping to lay a new kitchen floor; or Marilyn, the New Jersey neighbor who asked where the island tennis courts were located; or Marie, who came to Gotts Island wearing a dress and thus inappropriately attired was almost left on the dock at Bass Harbor because Russie Gott had a confirmed sense that a dress was not appropriate apparel for a proper "island person."

The kitchen floor has been refinished once again since Sam's visit, and the room now has a bright white new ceiling as well, but the woodstove—or at least the exact replica thereof—and the bleached out oak table by the window all remain in place. "When houses come undone, it is usually through a vague combination of disrepair and memory lapse," Akiko Busch has astutely written in *Geography of Home*. Disrepair there certainly was in our Gotts Island house—and it's still far from perfect—but the people, the structure of the house, field, stone, and sea all conspire to prevent the undoing of memory. Whatever skeins come loose can be rewoven in another pattern.

The island includes the sounds and images of people both living and dead. Even the dogs live here as ghosts in fact and in memory, joining a large company that includes our own family and friends, those who inhabited the house in generations that preceded us, those who came as summer people long before us, our neighbors who are the progeny of those first rusticating families. Some are regular summer residents, others brief visitors, but however short the time, they leave something of themselves. The island is a gathering. It is a site for undertaking the archaeology of memory. It is the perfect medium.

Unexpected Arrivals

The house was already full on the day Richard made his un-announced arrival. Even a big house can be full. And none of the guests had been invited. Well, not in any real way. There had been just a casual "you must come up to the island sometime," the kind of statement one makes when the time is preferably far off. And since the island is not exactly easy to get to and arrangements usually have to be made for a boat, we felt secure about controlling the guest flow.

But we were wrong. The "sometime" came, and not when we were expecting it. I remember it as a terrible summer. I was in graduate school, working over the summer months on an independent reading course in the eighteenth-century novel. Day after day, I got up at 5 a.m. to pore over hundreds of pages of *Clarissa*, *Tristram Shandy*, *Tom Jones*, *Robinson Crusoe*, and eight other big novels. By the time I had to get the wood stove going and breakfast started for the rest of the family, I had already put in three good hours of work. So it went, every day, seven days a week, from late June through July and into August.

Now it was late August, and it seemed that I would actually accomplish the huge task. I could take some reprieve from my labors for my last four days on the island. Desperately I looked forward to these days that would be my only "vacation" time that summer.

But again, I was wrong. Glancing out the kitchen window I saw a lean figure just coming round the curve of the path by Jane Holmes's wild rose hedge. The figure moved with a slow stalking gait, as if thrusting himself into each new step. The walk was unmistakable.

"O my goodness, it's Richard."

Two days earlier a similar scene had played out: "O my goodness, here's Uncle John just coming round the path by Jane Holmes's rose bushes, and Aunt Betty—and who *are* all those people who could only be coming here?"

That group turned out to include, in addition to Uncle John and Aunt Betty, their daughter Jane, and Jane's two young daughters. Jane, who lived with her parents, had what my family delicately called "emotional problems": she was, I see in retrospect, probably schizophrenic and was known to have an affinity for fire.

On the day when I caught sight of Richard making his way toward our house, we were all gathered round the big pine table having lunch: John, Chris, Ben, my mother, and the five members of my uncle's family. We were ten, and soon, with Richard's arrival, would be eleven. So much for four days vacation.

My mother made clear her view that any regret about having to plan (on an island with no store and in a house with no refrigerator) and prepare (on a wood stove) all the meals for eleven people was an act of extreme selfishness on my part: I should happily fulfill my obligation to her brother and his family. In short, relatives had to be accommodated. This seemed to me an outrageous position to take, but I was in fact very fond of my Uncle John, a highly literate man with a Scottish wit and burr to match, and left-wing politics first developed when he was a ship builder on the Clyde Bank. Besides, Vinie Moore had no doubt cooked on the wood stove for more people than this.

It was of course Richard who made the difference: the proverbial straw. Richard made a difference whenever and wherever he went. His unexpected visit at the island was a nightmare. He lost no time in establishing himself as the important guest to whom all must defer. All dinnertime conversation must perforce yield to his lectures on the French Revolution, which were addressed of course only to John, the fellow historian. He competed with all four children for attention and insulted everyone else.

I was furious. But I was usually furious with Richard. He had stalked into our lives at a university departmental reception about ten years before, and he remained with us, importantly in our consciousness, for more than two decades. "I could write the book on Richard," I used to say. But where to start? The Gotts Island visit came somewhere in the middle of the long history. When I heard of his death, years later, in a small town in Oregon where his life had finally taken him, I felt what seemed a slight sense of relief. I had in fact forgotten about the "book," about all the stories. But suddenly they came back, transformed into chapters in a life that was now over.

"He's the most brilliant historian of his generation," John would say; "an incredible researcher, an unusual imagination." We did not particularly notice that Richard drank a lot more than any of our other friends. Nor did we ever know exactly why, after only one year of teaching in the United States, he went back to Oxford to finish his D.Phil. there. We only guessed that it must have had something to do with his insufferable arrogance toward everyone, colleagues both senior and junior.

About a year after Richard's departure from the United States, we found ourselves in Oxford, in a large semi-detached house on the Woodstock Road rented from an eminent historian who happened to be John's department chair. Richard was now attached to a bright young Oxford graduate student in literature. But by early spring, that relationship was strained, and Richard needed a place to live. We had an extra room in the Woodstock Road house, and we could use a bit of extra income. Richard came to live with us, supposedly to pay board and a portion of the not inconsiderable rent. But again, the plan did not work out: Richard knowingly gave us worthless checks for his share of the rent, and I was subjected to embarrassing encounters at the local bank.

"Don't forget to stop by the college cellars and pick up more port," he would cheerily call out to me. Presaging his death from lung cancer thirty years later, the ever present aroma of his Gauloise drifted out of his room and down the staircase.

It's now several years since Richard's death in relative obscurity, his potential never fulfilled. My mother, Uncle John, Aunt Betty, and their daughter Jane all died well over a decade ago. Russie Gott, who brought my Uncle John and his family to the island that August day, died the same year as Ben. The intervening years have seen a return to the more normal pattern: we have had no unexpected visitors. We usually know who is coming. We make the arrangements; and Lyford Stanley, Russie's successor, is not likely to bring over to the island those whose names are not already on a small bit of paper thrust into his pocket.

Our friends take plans seriously. The island seems remote, the trip thither arduous. That is, it's more remote to the living. As for the others, those visitors of the past, they are somehow always there, at their worst or at their best. They still sit round the table, their voices absorbed into the very walls and sinew of the house.

Halibut

It was always halibut on the Friday night, the first night of Lance and Marjorie's annual three-day visit to the island. Usually broiled with just a bit of lemon and oil. Lance and Marjorie would drive up from Boston, buy the halibut from the fish dealer who parked his van on the road just out of Ellsworth, and be on the dock at Bass Harbor around 4:30. I usually baked a berry cake or pudding (but never pie: that was John's task on Saturday) and prepared the salad greens from Rita Kenway's garden. Sometimes, if it was both high tide and good weather, John and I might take our own boat over to pick up the visitors. On one particularly blustery day, with the seas chopping away, Lance and Marjorie sat stoically in the boat, with nary a trace of anxiety, carefully diverting the conversation to matters other than drownings at sea. We arrived at the island soaked to the bone, all four. Marjorie hated small boats too.

The halibut was Marjorie's special contribution. Unlike me, she was a genius at broiling halibut. It was always done to perfection, still moist in the middle. Our role as hosts never extended beyond advice on the vagaries of the stove; the rest was up to Marjorie. The halibut dinner was important because it was the start of our ritualized weekend. It never seemed odd that the arriving guest be in charge of the first dinner. That was just the way it worked out. Once in place, the tradition was never questioned.

I'm wondering now why we never took a photograph of the halibut dinner. We photographed ourselves having drinks on the deck before dinner, doing the annual tramp around Little Gotts Island, gathering mussels by Philip Moore's old weir, doing a puppet show for the island children with the

old 1960s puppet theatre with the peace sign. And we always took the shot of the special Saturday night, dress-up,
lobster dinner. But we didn't photograph the halibut.

We first met Lance and Marjorie in our graduate student
days at Stanford. Lance already had his D.Phil. from Oxford
and was in charge of the Western Civ program where John
taught in his last year of graduate school. Marjorie was both
a graduate student and the mother of two young children.
In the mid-sixties, being a wife and mother as well as a
graduate student, and having a nanny in her employ, placed
Marjorie in a different category from most of the graduate
student wives. Although we had children of similar ages, I
hardly knew Marjorie in those days. I only remember that
she and Lance were the most attractive couple I had ever
seen. He was handsome, she beautiful in a classic mode that
would always be with her. It was my loss that I didn't know
them better in those days.

Then the graduate school years ended. We went East.
Lance and Marjorie, we heard through the Stanford grape-
vine, remained in the West for several more years. It was
years later, when all the children were pretty much grown
or at least into young adulthood, that we heard again from
Lance and Marjorie. We received a formal card announcing
that they would be spending the 1982–83 academic year
in Princeton, where we were living. They were by then
independent scholars, based in Boston, and just recently
returned from a research year in Paris. We remet them at a
dinner party in Princeton and there recommenced, or, in a
sense began for the first time, our friendship. At some time
in the spring, we invited them to join us at Gotts Island that
summer.

So it began, the ritual of three-day summer visits. "We'll never stay longer than three days," Marjorie declared: "It's the old saw about fish and guests. More than three days and both begin to stink." It was always a Friday–Monday schedule. Lance and Marjorie stayed, in those early visits, in the old room with twin beds in the main house. They never complained about the lumpy beds and crumbling plaster or the fact that every movement could be heard from below. They entered into and enjoyed all the idiosyncrasies of a nineteenth-century house just barely making it into the twentieth.

It was a friendship of midlife, of people whose children are no longer vacationing with them. It was a friendship that came into our lives when we had the time to develop it. Lance and Marjorie were consummate good guests. "You should write the book on guest-ing," John used to tell them. It was so true.

They loved the island. We loved the island. They remembered all our stories about it. They added some of their own. We talked about history, about people we had all known, about kids and, ultimately, grandkids. One summer, when Ben happened to be with us too, they listened patiently to his enthusiastic accounts of flying, sharing the pleasure just as they did in all situations. They were like family. At that terrible moment when we heard the news of Ben's death in Africa, they were among the first people we called. Lance spoke at the memorial service in Princeton and he and Marjorie remained stalwart supports during those awful weeks. Four years later when Chris and Kathy were married at the island, Lance and Marjorie were at the rehearsal dinner helping to represent our family.

I don't know when the dress-up lobster dinners began, but I think it was the first year. Sometimes we found old clothes in the house; sometimes Lance brought the white flannel "bags" (trousers) that he had worn in his Oxford days. We moved the gate-leg table from the kitchen into the living room. If the weather was cool enough, we lit the fire. We got out the best candles and best paper napkins. John baked the blueberry pie. We served the best wine we had. We prepared ourselves for the annual photograph. There we are, four middle-aged people all dressed up in an old house on an island in Maine. We pose ourselves, the camera ticks on automatically; we smile and wait for the flashing red light.

Written for the memorial service for Marjorie Milbank Farrar, Cambridge, Massachusetts, March 2000.

Island Women

"That is no country for old men"
W. B. Yeats, "Sailing to Byzantium"

In important ways, the island is no country for the old. The rocks, high grasses, slippery paths, are not kind to those who do not see well or move easily; the houses with their ever pressing needs—weatherbeaten roofs, idiosyncratic plumbing, recalcitrant pumps—incessantly demand the attention of those strong and capable enough to give it. These are the constants. For a community of islanders who for the most part see one another only in the summer, each year is a marker, a milestone felt or observed in the bone. Gotts Island is no Byzantium, no place where we can aspire, like Yeats, to transcend time, to take ourselves, as he says, "out of nature."

But even if the island affirms time and reality, it may still be a country for old women. It is a place of strong women; it has ever been so. And strong island women have a special relationship to time and age. When I think of the generation preceding my own, of the women who were part of my own experience of the island, none of them fits the category of the old as conventionally understood in our mainland world. There are no "senior citizens" on the island. There are only people who are part of the place, and though their bodies age physically, their roles remain intact. As long as they are on the island, they are who they are—who they always were. We expect them to live up to their roles; and they do. Even as island ghosts, free literally of nature and human time, they continue those roles for us the living.

JEAN

It seemed to us that Jean had always been there. Every summer. In the years after her retirement from the library at Macalaster College in St. Paul, she spent the entire summer at the island, flying to Bangor, picking up a car she garaged in Maine, always following a carefully orchestrated routine. By the time we arrived, Jean would usually be well established in her house, the one closest to ours, on the top of the hill. She would be the first to welcome us, standing in the kitchen door while John was still working to install the screen that had been stored in the barn for the winter. I'd worry about the mosquitoes while we talked.

The time came when Jean could not make the trip from St. Paul to the island. "She's in a home, a senior citizen facility," her son told us. He and his wife do not live in Jean's old house; they have built their own cottage, large, new and modern, on the north side of the island, away from the village.

Jean suffers from Alzheimer's, they say. But she has not forgotten everything. She has not forgotten the island. It was a terrible moment when the family had to tell her she could not go to Gotts Island. She had come every year since the 1920s when she was a young child. First her family were boarders, then they had bought the house she now owns. Her life moments have been counted through summers on the island. "I remember when that large spruce in your field was a stripling," she used to tell us. I look up at the now towering tree and think of her words.

This year Jean's house stands empty. It sits, waiting: for the grasses to be cut, porch furniture put out, garden tended,

"The offshore islands belong to themselves" ——*Ruth Moore*

Houses long gone, a village of the absent

floors swept, shades raised up. It is now full summer, and
no one is there. The lupine in the field behind Jean's house
have come and are now almost gone, pale stalks remaining,
seeds straining against the pods to burst and fall into the
receptive soil.

HARRIET

It was the week of 9/11. I was home nursing injuries I had
received from an errant skateboarder who had run into me
on my steep street in Berkeley, when my niece, my sister's
daughter, called from Massachusetts with the news.

I never receive calls from my niece.

"Has something happened to your mother?" I asked in
alarm.

"No," she said. "It's Harriet. She died yesterday."

I'm looking at photographs from Harriet's last summer on
the island. I see her there in the audience we reassembled
for the first Gotts Island puppet show in a decade. Our
neighbor Carl brought her up the hill in his golf cart–*cum*
personal taxi. There is no golf at Gotts Island, but there are
people needing rides and goods needing transport. Harriet
sat comfortably in the golf cart that day. But Harriet always
looked comfortable. Once she came to an impromptu dinner at our house wearing pajamas and a bathrobe. "I'd love
to come if I can come as I am," she had said when I invited
her. She did look rather strange, but she was comfortable.
And so were we.

I think I must have met Harriet in the mid-sixties when she
came up with her then teen-aged children to stay with her

aunt, Miss Caroline Holmes. "Aunt C" owned the house
that Harriet later inherited. But through many of the years
of my own children's growing up, Harriet lived in Bermu-
da and only came to the island in the spring or fall. The
house—Aunt C. having died by then—was usually rented.
It's the series of renters I remember in those years. Harriet's husband, Kennedy, was spoken of but seemed always a
mystery in that period. "He doesn't like the island," I was
told. "He came once when he first married Harriet, hated
it, and never came back."

But Kennedy did come back. And so did Harriet. They were
retired by then. Harriet was of the generation who always
referred to her Smith classmates, circa Class of 1938, as the
"girls." She sometimes wore a jacket that went back to her
Northampton days. When Chris married a Smith alumna
almost sixty years later, Harriet, complete with hat and a
heavy slathering of sun protector cream on her nose, joined
a photograph with the younger graduates. I always think of
Harriet with that thick coating of white cream on her nose,
strange hats and sexy sandals that looked so out of place
on Gotts Island. She told stories of coming up to the island
from New Jersey as a child, taking the steamer from New
York; she described being a young wife in California right
after World War II. She never spoke of years of fighting de-
pression. She almost never mentioned the daughter who
had died in a car accident in her early twenties.

Harriet chatted about people living and dead, stories old
and new. She knew the gossip. She was the center of things.
And so was her house. Kennedy, handsome and still with
the look of a man who had gone to Princeton and studied
Law at Yale, made the drinks and served them up with Tris-

cuits and sharp cheddar from HG Reed's store in Bass Harbor. We all sat around in Harriet's living room, the prettiest room on Gotts Island, painted pale blue like the sea on a slightly misty day. On the wall was a portrait of Harriet herself as a girl of about twelve. She wore a blue dress and her hair was tied with a creamy satin bow.

I loved that living room. From the window seat on the west wall, her favorite spot, Harriet looked down into the middle and inner pools, the bar between them and the bay beyond. I still see her sitting on her blue cushioned window seat, smoking cigarettes, reading, I imagine, just as the child in the portrait had done so many years ago. How many changes of the tide Harriet must have witnessed from her window seat perch. How many times must she have watched the sea scud in around the pebbly bar and then rush out to reveal once again the empty contours of the pool.

"Shorten It Up"

Sometimes we hear the voices of the past in ways we are not expecting. Fragments of language live through time. Then they surface in new contexts, bringing with them traces of their own history.

"Shorten it up," Lyford good-naturedly said to Vince, who was in the middle of a rather long story.

We four—our Australian visitors Rhys and Colleen, John, and I—were Vince's audience. And we had plenty of time for a tale of some length. We were on vacation, just standing around by Uncle Mont's house, listening to Vince, nodding at the right moments, signaling our attention. Vince never expected much verbal response. He himself would supply all the words. We felt easy, lulled by the story told in Vince's Rhode Island accent.

Lyford, whose family has been on and around the offshore islands of Blue Hill Bay since the eighteenth century, is a man of few words. And right at that moment he needed Vince's attention for a pressing matter. He couldn't wait for the not-yet-in-sight end of Vince's story. He had a tide to catch, a trip to Bass Harbor to make, someone's freight to bring over.

So he said, "Shorten it up."

And Vince, with similar good nature, did.

I doubt that any of the four of us remembers now what Vince's story was about. But Lyford's "shorten it up" has stayed with us. "Shorten it up," we say to one another when our own stories seem overly involved and lengthy (a not infrequent occurrence). The phrase has come to stand in for our friendship, a verbal cue that brings back the pleasure of the days we spent together at the island.

"Shorten it up" has a place in our lives, a private language among friends. And we thought, wrongly of course, that in some way it belonged to us. We didn't know it had a history, one we could have found in Dr. Small's *History of Swan's Island, Maine.*

Dr. Small devotes a good part of his *History* to the fisheries of Swans Island, citing the personal account of one Aaron Lightfoot to take us back to a world of hand-line mackerel fishing in the nineteenth century. It is the voice of Lightfoot that describes "handling cold, wet lines and colder, wetter fish," an experience that is nothing short of "diabolical." It is Lightfoot who portrays the chill of the dark, then the misery of daylight finally dawning amidst cold pouring rain. And finally, Lightfoot comes to the climax:

> With the first movement of the captain's arm indicating the presence of fish, everybody rushed madly to the rail, and jigs are heard on all sides splashing into the water, and eager hands and arms are stretched at their full length over the side, feeling anxiously for a nibble . . .
>
> "*Shorten it up*", says the skipper, and we shorten our lines to about eight feet from the rail to the hooks . . . [ital. mine]

"Shorten it up," the captain said. It all makes sense. Had I not heard Lyford use the phrase that summer day, I prob-

ably would not even have noticed it in Dr. Small's *History*.
But now the captain's "shorten it up" leaps from the page. I
know that language; Lyford speaks it. It is still with us. Perhaps Lyford's antecedents were among the fishermen who
heard that command as daylight dawned on a day one hundred fifty years ago. Perhaps when he told Vince to wrap up
his story, to "shorten it up," he spoke from some inchoate
connection with that skipper, with those men.

But even if it is true, we could not have seen the connection
that day in July. We were simply enjoying an afternoon of
brilliantly warm sunshine at Gotts Island with Swans far off
in the distance. We took the language as it came, were satis-
fied to experience its efficacy. We knew nothing of the lives
for whom "shorten it up" was no figure of speech, those for
whom it served, rather, a practical function grounded in
day to day labor. We had no inkling of a wintry dawn, cold
drenching rain, freezing fingers, and an ongoing struggle to
extract mackerel from a turbulent sea.

Later I wanted to ask Lyford if he was aware of the history
of his own phrase. He may well have been. But Lyford, as I
have said, is a man of few words. Every word counts. Meta-
language, I expect, would never be his cup of tea.

So I said nothing and waited to tell the story in my next e-
mail to Rhys and Colleen in Melbourne. "Shorten it up," I
wrote on the subject line.

Going to the Dogs

The dogs too belong, literally, to an archaeology of the island's past. In *The Indian Shell Heap: Archaeology of the Ruth Moore Site*, a small monograph on the Gotts Island shell heap named in honor of Ruth Moore, canine remains play an important role:

> We cannot be sure what kind of human behaviors and attitudes toward dogs the canine remains represent . . . The [dog-eating] ceremony, which occurred among both Iroquois and New England Algonkian tribes, indicates that dogs not only had economic value, but also embodied spiritual values such as courage that the warriors ritually partook of by eating their flesh.

But we didn't really need archaeologists to tell us that dogs go with islands: small dogs that have to lifted from the boat to the dock, big dogs that jump out of the skiff and rush to the shore shaking water on to anyone or anything that happens to be there. Anyone living on Gotts Island knows this. That dogs have always gone with islands, that some 1500 years ago they held "high value as pets, hunting companions, and perhaps as a form of wealth," may confound but not surprise; and if the so-called "spiritual values" thought to be conferred by dogs to the warriors who ate them are obscure, we do not question the possibility.

Nor is it the business of archaeologists to tell us about contemporary human behaviors and attitudes toward dogs. The relationships among dogs and people, particularly on small islands, remain complex.

"Ralph's dogs bit me," shouted Vince, holding up his bandaged hand in the middle of the Cozy Cove restaurant in Southwest Harbor. In the summer Vince and his wife, Dot Gott, live in Uncle Mont's cottage a few hundred yards from the Indian shell heap where the dog remains were found.

We had just arrived in Maine that day when we saw Vince in the Cozy Cove. We hadn't even been out to the island yet. But of course we knew the voice that boomed across the no-smoking zone. Even at seventy-five, Vince was a huge man, strong enough to carry our old Empress Atlantic wood stove single-handedly right out the kitchen door.

Dot was born in Uncle Mont's old house, the red cottage with the steeply pitched roof that sits by the pool and dock. But the real point is that all Gotts Island traffic and all dogs—walking properly on their leashes, or just tearing around in a doggie way, peeing on groceries and gear coming on or going off the island—pass by Dot and Vince's door.

Vince does not like dogs. It's not that he's a cat person, like the other Gotts Islanders who are hostile to dogs; he just doesn't see any value, spiritual or otherwise, in dogs. He especially doesn't like the three dogs that belong to Ralph's household: a pleasant collie mix, a large but unthreatening husky, and a small schnauzer. Most of us think the two larger dogs are just fine, but the small schnauzer is, well, a schnauzer. Irascible. It was, of course, Niles, the schnauzer, that bit Vince.

Vince was holding up for our inspection his bandaged hand. Niles had made, to put it mildly, an impression. And it was an event that apparently had had repercussions. Vince, I was later told, had threatened to shoot Ralph's dogs if he ever saw them running loose around his house again; and the argument, according to local gossip, was an especially heated one, replete with angry threats.

But as it turned out, no dog was shot. In the usual way of things, the turmoil abated. Still, perhaps Mrs. Babbidge, one of the original Gotts Islanders, was right when she told Hilda Kenway, a summer person from Boston to whom she was selling her house in 1928, that there was so much fighting on Gotts Island she thought the whole island should just disappear into the sea. Atlantis indeed.

That was enough for one summer. The next year the dog disputes continued with the same cast of characters and the addition of a few visitors like a basset hound named Bentley whom I met one morning just as he was being evicted from Rita Kenway's vegetable garden. Bentley, ears a-flapping, an enthusiastic expression on his droopy face, was the guest of Carl Taplin's basset, Zack, who is older and more lethargic, little motivated to pursue nimble footed cats or dig in Rita's garden. The worst sin attributed to Zack is that, with his low stature, he chases deer and nips their genitals (their "privates" one local resident says), a most unpleasant practice whatever anatomical term one uses. But I really don't think that Zack is capable of such athletic endeavors.

The next year too, the incorrigible Niles was tied in his yard. That stopped the biting—at least of anyone beyond the range of his line—but it exacerbated the barking and yapping, which began each morning about 5:15 a.m., causing furor in every bedroom round about. "We need those dog-eating warriors," I mumbled crossly to John as I buried my head more deeply into the pillows. There's no doubt about it: the petulant Niles is not popular. Even the people who are not especially fond of one another are united in their dislike of Niles.

But Niles is not alone in the annals of island dogdom. There was the infamous Lucky, Betty Baldwin's terrier, the evocation of whose memory sounded the only negative note at Betty's memorial service on the island. I remember the evening in 1963 when Lucky made a sizable gouge in my mother's thigh. Others had similar stories. "And we have Lucky's paw prints on the rafters of our house," volunteered Tina Wiener Bell at the memorial. "He stepped on the lumber with muddy paws and no one thought to clean up the marks." Thus has Lucky achieved local fame and immortality.

Thirty years later, Carl Taplin's pointer-mix, Butchie, predecessor of Zack, became the dog of note, the last of the big-time biters and most famous for a wound inflicted on Valerie Beaman as she walked up the town road past Butchie's house. The stricken Valerie wasn't even on Butchie's property. But unlike Lucky or Niles, Butchie was a complex creature: he could be agreeable, accommodating, smart. With Butchie, one wanted to forgive and forget the dreaded fault. A Berkeley child visiting us some years ago still remembers happily the evening that Butchie and Carl came for dinner, and Butchie leapt up to retrieve treats from the *top* of the kitchen door. It was an impressive performance; Butchie, clearly pleased with his accomplishment, grinned broadly.

It was two days after Betty's memorial and the recitation of the Lucky stories that the subject of Butchie came up over at Carl's house. I was surprised because we always try to stay away from discussion of Butchie when we are Carl's guests. But that evening Carl had Butchie on his mind. He seemed to need to talk about him, to retrieve his presence, to tell us how much he loved that dog and what their years together had meant.

"He understood so much," Carl was telling us. "In the end he was smart enough to know that the game was up. That's why he killed himself by deliberately running in front of that truck in Northeast Harbor."

Butchie had committed suicide? His death was no accident? Butchie had *willed* to die?

The living room grew darker as the evening advanced. The circle of guests drew closer together. And more surprises were to come.

"But he's still here, you know," Carl went on.

His face brightened. The quiescent Zack gave a snore from his corner. Carl reached up to the shelf over the solar powered cd player, and took down what looked like a coffee canister. He shook it like a large castanet.

We heard a clinking sound like gravel on metal.

"Here he is," said Carl.

CR

At the Abbe Museum, the bones of those early Gotts Island dogs, the forebears of Lucky, Niles, and Butchie, are silent. They lie peacefully in their glass case. There are five in all.

"Ernie," the archaeologists' favorite, found as buried, "with a large flat rock on his chest," just below the layer dated as 1500–2000 years ago; "Bert," second best in state of preservation, terrier sized; and Ernie and Bert's three companions, found only in fragments.

These were all small dogs, probably about Niles's size. They had spent a long time at Gotts Island, curled up comfortably (except, perhaps, for the flat rock on the chest) in their beds of coarsely crushed shell. Whatever their lives had been, whatever they had experienced themselves or represented to their long disappeared owners, they had been in the right place: safe in their shelly layer, impervious to time, the relentless beat of the ocean against the shore, and the tremors of the human world.

5

PATHWAYS

Going Places

It takes only one path to locate a house on a small island, but our house has three. With no roads to compete with, left to themselves, the paths head west, north, and east respectively. Sometimes they take us along to unseen destinations, sometimes they reveal what we have not noticed before. But wherever they go, they provide connections, with the island and with other lives, past and present.

The westward path is the major one. Following the orientation of the house, it leads to the properties of our closest neighbors, to the cemetery, and finally to the shore and the dock. It is the route of arrivals and exits. Like an extra-long front walk, the path allows us to see who is coming before they reach our kitchen door; we catch our last sight of visitors as they disappear down the path close by the cemetery fence.

In an early family photo, Chris, a toddler, stands in the path eating a blueberry he has just picked from an adjacent bush; in another, Chris and Kathy, in wedding finery, run joyously up the path just at the point where Chris had stood thirty years before. And in yet another photograph, taken earlier on that same wedding day, John, Chris, and I carry a large antique pitcher of bright blue delphinium down the path toward Ben's grave. The path shares our summer lives almost as much as the house to which it connects. It places events, whether small or momentous, in time and space. And it places us.

Though proceeding with straightforward determination down the hill, the path heading west is not easy to see as it crosses the Kenways' always carefully mowed and clipped yard. Only on a wet or damp day, or in early morning dew, will the footsteps in the grass be clearly marked, revealing in relief the way the walker has taken. We do not stray far from the indentation, however slight, that marks a well-used route of passage.

Once past the town road crossing, there is no mistaking what is path and what is field. The way, now dipping sharply down toward the pool, is deeply indented, clearly demarcated. Ruth Moore called it the "wheelworn rut that a hundred years of grass had failed to fill." But from our house—Ruth's house—the "rut" disappears from view just past the cemetery as if, like all those who use it, it has business of its own.

Perhaps all paths have, delineate, or demand, determination. Perhaps this is the nature of paths. They determine where we will go, speaking with the authority of generations of walkers who have preceded us. New paths, like those made by the snowmobiles or hunters, have no such authority. And they tend to grow over soon, forgotten.

Old paths carry within them some secret knowledge of the land and history that will be ever closed off to us. They remind us of mysteries we will never fathom. What voices have been heard on the path? What sorrows or anguish or joy were experienced by those who walked the path? What preoccupations, thoughts, schemes, or plans were mulled over in these passage places? What earnest conversations—talk of love, life, work, family, future joys, illness, or death?

The path that runs west from the house to the shore signals mainland preoccupations, plans for a day ashore, errands to be fetched, some of them crucial. Susanna Gott informs us in a diary entry written in the summer of 1852 that Mr. Moore has gone to fetch the doctor for his wife, Asenath, and adopted daughter, Judith Cates. I imagine the first Captain Moore hastening down the path toward the pool on a desperate mission to seek the medical help that would not keep either of the women from dying before winter frost. Asenath Moore's funeral was, according to the diarist, the largest she had known at the island. Boats brought mourners from Bass Harbor for the occasion. Having landed at the dock, they would have walked up the path to the cemetery from the dock. The Moores, the Gotts, the others, would, like ourselves on the day we buried Ben's ashes, have walked down.

We need not walk westward of course. Three paths provide choices. It's just that the limits seem more clear on a small island. I can walk or jog only so far. And then the path will return me to the departure point. The house at the intersection of paths is both a beginning and a terminus.

The path that meanders east begins behind the house, enters our woodlot just past the eastern edge of our ever-diminishing field, and then scrabbles across the ledges that dominate this part of the island's normally shady interior. Once past the stony outcropping, the path traverses the marshy area behind the old Strauss well, and finally arrives at the enormous granite rocks that border the sea. On an

island all paths lead to the sea—or to another path that
borders the shore. The sea defines the land, ultimately determining the routes through which we read and chart the
terra firma.

Like lemmings, we follow the paths to the sea, whether
Blue Hill Bay on the west, the westward passage to the
north, or the open ocean to the east and the south. The path
to the meadow runs north from our house, marks a right-
of-way between two neighboring properties, and heads directly to the Silvers' farmhouse. It then loops slightly to
the west to avoid the house itself, picks up its original direction, and shambles downhill through dark woods. The
path is rocky and rutty as it makes its descent, the crooked
trees and old stone walls pressing close. Here and there one
finds a few random bricks, worn with age now, the residue,
Russie Gotts always said, of moving what is now the Silvers' farmhouse from its original spot in the meadow to its
present site up the hill in the trees. "Too much weather in
the meadow," Russie declared, though the house, then the
property of Enoch Moore, had been moved well before his
lifetime.

Crossing a margin from dark to light, the path enters with
a burst the broad meadow that is the island's northernmost
point. It's as if we open an invisible door and enter a new
and different space, luminous on a sunny morning, with
the waters of the westward passage and the Bass Harbor
light clearly visible beyond. Before me, the path pursues
its sinuous way, a rod-wide swath through the red grasses,
curling its way north and then turning abruptly to the east
where the brilliantly glowing grasses and the still ripening blueberries end, and only a narrow hunter's route, now

heavily overgrown, penetrates heavy forest. The path has led me to a place that is open and enclosed at the same time. Defined and seemingly bounded. I avoid the hunter's dark route into the trees and retrace my steps back toward the village and my own house. Once again I will cross the margin, this time from light into dark.

The town road, its longest segment bisecting the island, holds a unique place on the island. A dirt and stony track, it begins in what was once the village, ultimately traverses from west to east the spruce forested interior of the island, turns into a narrow path at the island's narrow neck, and ends at the granite promontory where the foundation of Miss Peterson's house silently stands. The town road is linear; it does not meander. Although I don't know the exact route taken by Katherine Crosby, the *Boston Globe* writer who came to "cover" Miss Peterson's story, I always imagine it was the town road. The narrative of the journalist marches right along, as if determined by the very linearity of the town road.

But the town road is different in other ways as well. Unlike the other island paths, it is called, literally, a "road," and at least until it reaches the neck, it's broad enough to accommodate a jeep or a truck. Roads are not paths: roads go somewhere, and unlike paths, their function may be to disconnect as much as to connect. Notably, the town road is never called the island road. Until recent times, it was maintained, at least in theory, by Tremont Township on the mainland; in a sense it seemed to belong to the town, to an "away," and was to this degree always other.

Perhaps this is why the town road has been a continuing topic of discussion and disagreement at Gotts Island. There

are no conflicts over paths, only over the road, which is
in no way suited to construction and other vehicles, but
which, with ongoing building and rehab projects, has been
pressed into service. The refusal of some islanders even
to consider the problem of upkeep of the road may stem
from a kind of denial: they want the road to be the footpath
which, to most of us, it is. When the town of Tremont gave
over responsibility for road maintenance to the local island
residents—a properly designated road has to meet certain
standards, and to prohibit the popular, and necessary, island
atv's—the main transportation route of the island became
a major issue. According to mainland thinking, a road is ultimately defined by its capacity, or lack thereof, to accommodate vehicles. But we are, essentially, an island of people
who want to walk on paths.

But there are places where we don't need a path. At the
furthermost eastern margin of the island, the site of Miss
Peterson's ill-fated house, the granite forms a massive
flat terrace marked by the broken husks of sea urchins
and bleached gull droppings. I can walk easily here, moving briskly along on a natural promenade that defines the
shore. There is no determined route beyond that dictated
by stone. I leave no footprint, no trace, on these massive
rocks; and perhaps for that reason there is comfort in returning once again to the more yielding path that will return me to the village and the house.

The traces are on the paths, not on the unrelenting border
with the sea, but in the soft mosses, the lichen shrouded
outcroppings, the rectangular foundations that occupy
dark, secret thickets. I know the boundaries of this island
I inhabit each summer. And knowing the circumference is

important: to go round, to "encompass" the space, is, in a sense, to possess it. But I know the island's curves, inlets, coves, and promontories because I know the paths. The two go together. Perhaps more than any other geographical formation, the very boundedness of the small island relates our bodies to the ground that we mark with our feet. The paths that circle, traverse, or simply meander over the island enable the relationship.

Yet the path always keeps something to itself. I feel this in the places where it crosses the stark border from bright field to dark spruce forest, where horizon and distance disappear, and vision is occluded. But even when I jog along the meadow path on a brilliantly sunny morning, when the field and grasses unfold in their immediacy before me, my knowledge is partial. That elemental knowing that comes with living in a small, seemingly defined place, a kind of topographical knowing, is never complete. In years of visiting Gotts Island there are undoubtedly acres of overgrown brush, sticky bogs, and thick tangles of vines that I have never seen. The path, literally, will not reveal them to me.

The path determines the order in which we move through and experience physical space, but it also leaves space for filling in. It allows us to bring something of ourselves to the enterprise. In *A Book of Migrations*, Rebecca Solnit speaks of metaphor as the "transportation system of the mind, the way we make connections between disparate things." The paths and tracks that connect us to our neighbors, to the other parts of the island, to the surrounding sea—in motion and pause, darkness and light—all invite a "transporting," a process of making connections.

This means that the authority of the path is not absolute. We have freedom, should we desire it, even to move out of our ordinary selves. Virginia Woolf spoke of walking as shedding "the self our friends know us by and [becoming] part of that republican army of anonymous trampers, whose society is so agreeable after the solitude of one's room." On a small island, we do "necessitous walking": we take down the mail, pick up the mail, walk to a neighbor's garden to get the zucchini and lettuce for dinner, walk to deliver messages to houses that have no telephones. But like Woolf, and the illustrious company of romantic walkers of an earlier generation—the writers like John Thelwall, Samuel Taylor Coleridge, Charles Lamb, or William Wordsworth—we ply the island paths as leisure walkers. We can distance ourselves from what we are seeing, and we can transform it so that it becomes part of our particular vision. We can engage in a special kind of "hunting and gathering" as we move along the path. We can go to many places.

No Trespassing

As I walked down the path toward the pool, I noticed that the high grasses in the field would have to be cut before the annual island Fourth of July baseball game could be played. But, I thought, the various relatives of the Parker family, who owned the field, would take care of it. They always did. Never a baseball player myself, I was on my way to take a swim.

I was moving swiftly, had just passed by the cemetery, and was approaching the spot where the alders are growing out so far that they block the view of the path ahead and the dock and the outer pool. I didn't expect to see anyone coming up the path from the dock, certainly not the Andersons. Everyone on the island knew that their son Ben had drowned in a lake in New Hampshire in May, but no one had said that they would be coming. They must have just arrived on the high tide. That's when people come on the island, especially if they have freight. Who wants to carry their canvas L. L. Bean bags, duffels, back packs, six-packs of beer—the whole lot—across the bar and the mud flats? The replacement for our old Empress Atlantic wood stove, the new refrigerator, shingles for the barn roof, the stone for our Ben's grave—all came on at the high tide.

Sue Anderson had always been a slim woman, the sort of person who in the early 1970s when I first met her seemed made for those long-skirted simple dresses I associated with photographs of Woodstock. I didn't really know how the Andersons happened to come to the island with their young children; but somehow they had gotten to know "young George," who was related to the Gotts; and

George, probably needing the money, sold them his camp in the woods.

The camp, small and primitive, was built up by the old bog where the islanders once gathered cranberries (not the little upland berries that I pick in the fields, but the kind that now come in the Ocean Spray can). I guess the Andersons must have liked Gotts Island a lot to buy George's camp; they didn't seem to mind that there was not even a glimpse of the ocean from the front door, or that for several years they had to share the place with George. The main point was just to be able to come to the island, even if they couldn't come very often or stay for long.

At some point the sharing deal ended, we hardly saw George on the island, and the Andersons stayed to join the rhythm of families coming back each summer, through all those years when children grow from toddlers to young adults and beyond. Their kids were younger than ours, I never knew them well, but I saw them grow up and I knew that my neighbor Harriet had been very happy when the Anderson boys, Ben and Jake, now young men, agreed to paint her house. The boys and their friends seemed to work hard on Harriet's house, and it certainly looked the better for it, sitting sparkling white in the field by the cemetery, just overlooking the sea.

It's a wonderful house—it even appeared on the cover of Sarah Orne Jewett's *Country of the Pointed Firs*—and the field, the smoothest on the island, is perfect for the annual Fourth of July baseball game. The Andersons' boys played. So did my son Ben, and the Parkers' nephew Brad. It was the day after the Fourth, in 1991, that our Ben went off to Africa and we said good-bye to him for what turned out to be the last time in the parking lot of the Cozy Cove restaurant in Southwest Harbor. The Andersons' Ben was still a young teenager then, and Brad wasn't angry at the neighbors.

It was July 3 when I suddenly saw the Andersons coming up the path by the cemetery. And I knew that their son Ben had drowned in that lake in New Hampshire, and I knew that I had not written to them. I told myself I did not know them well enough. But that wasn't the reason. I just couldn't tell them how well I knew what it meant to lose a son named Ben, and how, when I pass the cemetery fence, I think of that baseball game on the Fourth of July, 1991.

Nor could I explain why it seems so right that the cemetery is in the same field where the baseball game is played. The stones marking the graves are inside the white painted fence of course, and I've never known the ball to cross the fence. Even the strongest hitters can't do that. Our Ben's grave is pretty close to the fence on the side close to the baseball diamond, but I know that the ashes that traveled such a long way, all the way from Africa, to be buried there are safe. There's no question of where the boundaries of the cemetery are. We can ask why the Andersons' boy Ben drowned in that lake in New Hampshire and why our Ben was killed by a bird in a game park in Africa, but there's no debate about what's a cemetery and what is not. The big crows that sit on the finials of the fence posts every morning know that too.

I wasn't thinking of that, though, when I met the Andersons on the path, Bill's face wordlessly kind, Sue's, even thinner than I had remembered, grief marked in every line. I saw the dog first, a black lab, and in an instant, the two of them, just past that patch of alders where the sea comes into view again. The moment of recognition was so brief, the moment that had to lead to a greeting.

"I'm so glad you're here," I said. And I, who have never hugged the Andersons in more than twenty years of seeing them at Gotts Island, hugged Sue and Bill. "It can't be easy, but I'm glad you're here."

Yes, there was recognition. They knew. I knew. There are some things we don't have to say. Or, at least, not then, not with that pain charted on Sue's face. They were on their own mission. That was clear. I passed on, down the hill, to take my swim.

But the water felt particularly cold that day, and my tears were getting all mixed up with the incoming tide. It wasn't the shock of the cold. I had been swimming for more than thirty years in that pool, and cold water had never made me cry. No, I wept because I couldn't stop thinking about the children we lose, the baseball games that will not be played.

That's why the sign was so terrible. When I came up the path again, close by the cemetery fence, following the route that Sue and Bill had taken, my body still tingling from the cold, I saw it. The ugly, garish, orange sign read "No Trespassing." While I was down at the pool, someone had put it there, at the edge of the field by the cemetery. The sign seemed to contain within it a surfeit of resentment and anger—against family, neighbors, even life. Signs don't contain explanations. But the message was an outrage: to the sea and the sky, to the grasses, to memory.

Deserted Houses

On a dank gray day in June, I follow the familiar track that starts out as the town road. It's a route I have walked or jogged hundreds of times. But today, the third straight day of rain and penetrating cold, I am taking my first island walk of the year. Only the clumps of lilac, apple blossom, lupine, and columbine tell the season. I shiver under two sweaters and a parka. My boots squish through puddles in the deeply rutted spots on the town road. It's a day of muffled sound and obscured sight.

I'm doing the circuit, beating the bounds. I'm visiting houses where I know I will find nobody home. The houses await their summer inhabitants. Despite the sharp wind that signals otherwise, we are, after all, in the second week in June: opening up time. But the houses, still boarded, await warmth, a fire in woodstove or fireplace, and human companionship. In the meantime they sit lifeless, connected with neither the natural nor the human. Liminal.

As I pass the neck, the narrow place that joins the two bulbs of the island, I can just hear the sound of the booming surf at the eastern point of the island. It seems far away, but it's less than half a mile. This will be my first stop: the "box on the rocks," the house on the granite rocks that we rented so many years ago. The small gray cottage is much changed and improved under the present owners, but it still sits precariously atop the rocky shelf. Today, as I expected, its windows are boarded over, lifeless eyes. Waves crash in just yards from the front door. Remembering the summer more than forty years ago that we spent in this house, I ask myself yet again, "How did we ever live here with a toddler who had just learned to walk"?

Trespassing is rarely a problem on the island and certainly
not this early in the summer. But I still feel clandestine,
spy-like, an unseen presence. There is an element of excite-
ment and pleasure in having this secret. Perhaps I am a tres-
passer. But trespassing on what, on whom? The boarded up
house is impassive to my foot or my eye. It yields nothing. It
belongs to its winter, off-season world that I do not know.
What storms did this house witness in the winter just past?
What howling winds, bursts of salt spray, blizzarding snow?
I imagine. The important point is that the house has withstood whatever forces it had to contend with. It has survived. It waits for better days and in the meantime serves
my own imaginative wanderings.

If I climb back over the rocks I will rejoin the path that continues around the head and follows the edge of the massive
ledges of granite that stretch like a boardwalk along this
part of the island. Ordinarily I would take to the rocks at
this point; but today, in the rain, I won't trust the slippery
surface. I'll stay on the path where the grasses, the result
of weeks of rains, grow long and silky, lush green. The old
islanders say that this part of Gotts Island, the neck and the
smaller, easternmost, bulb, was once entirely pasture. It's
not hard to imagine the path I am following as the vestige
of that once-open, grazed, land. Back at the neck, a piece of
an old fence gate, marking off a pasture, is still visible.

I'm traipsing toward another house, the "brown house," an
arts and craft cabin built about 1904. Set back into the trees
but still close to the open sea, the long front porch of the
house commands a clear view of the great granite stretches
and the sea beyond. The porch has been newly renovated, I
see, strong and secure, the new lumber contrasting with the

old clapboard. The official name of this house is "Nowan-then." It seems that there is more "then" than "now": the porch is vacant, awaiting the old Adirondack rockers that will transform it from an empty stage to a lived space.

The path curls up and around the brown house, taking me back to the neck, and then to the shore on the southern side of the main part of the island. Near the neck, the path is clear, but each year moves it further back from the edge of the ever-eroding bluff. Ominous signs of the battle be-tween land and weather are everywhere here: chunks of rock-studded soil have fallen away and the gray remains of large trees that once grew on the bluff now lie upended, entangled in boulders, on the stony beach below. Jagged, twisted roots protrude from the steep face of the bluff, as if clutching vainly for life. With each succeeding year, the neck is becoming more narrow. I imagine a future century when Gotts will be cut in two, all the properties on the eastern side sitting on their own little island, apart from the main.

But I have other calls to make in this strange circuit of visi-tation. It's only a short way along the path, to Bella Strauss's house. Built close to the rocks on the south shore of the is-land, this house replaces Bella's father's sprawling log cabin that burned to the ground in 1960. I scramble down the rocky outcropping that once formed the dining room wall in the original Strauss cottage, the one that I visited as a child when my sister lived there. I remember breakfast in that strange dining room with a cliff face as a wall: a dark, cold, and mysterious space.

Each house has its story, perhaps especially so when nothing of the original structure remains. Unlike Miss Peterson's

house, no foundation stones mark the footprint of the old
Strauss house. But a woman died here too. No one knows
why Mr. Strauss's wife was not able to escape the house
with the others on the night when the fire broke out. And
by morning, according to all accounts, not a trace could
be found. Mr. Strauss never returned to Gotts Island, Bella
proceeded to build her new and much smaller cottage, and
in the usual way of things, the trees and brush grew up
around whatever was left of its large predecessor. In all the
years I have gone to Gotts Island as an adult, I have never
seen a single remnant of that house. This is an oddity on
an island where the foundation markers tend to remain as
mysterious reminders of the past. Another mystery.

Bella is gone now too, leaving the house to friends who use
it regularly in the summer. But on this dark, wet day, its
windows boarded, the house sits, like the others, lifeless
and desolate beside the granite border of the sea. Sloshing
past, I'm remembering Bella's asking me, in what turned
out to be her last summer on the island, to check in on her
when I went by on my morning jog. "Just to see that I'm
not toes-up in the kitchen," she said. It was all very mat-
ter-of-fact. Bella was, after all, a physician: no sentimental
nonsense about illness and death here. Fortunately I never
had to face the experience of finding her "toes up in the
kitchen." She died at her home in New Hampshire. Alas
poor Bella. I knew her well. And I miss her.

Once past Bella's house and its outbuildings, I'm in the old
track that continues along the shore and comes round to the
village again. The path here is a lake of dark mud and standing water, bordered by tall, lanky grasses. I'm in a bog. It's
amazing that Bella could drive her three-wheeler over this

track, dragging the small trailer that held her groceries and gear. She wore a bright parka and a visored cap with small wings over her ears. One of her series of huge dogs usually sat behind with the gear—or ran ahead, much to Bella's frustration, with wild, undisciplined energy. I remember the last one, an amiable Irish water spaniel who rushed out to greet all passersby. The day she asked me to check in on her in her kitchen Bella also gave me precise instructions on what to do with the dog in case of medical emergency involving herself. Interestingly, the directive for the dog was considerably more detailed than that for the owner.

Just a few more houses along the road now, a few more deep puddles. Here's the Berndts' house, and though empty of its inhabitants, its windows are not boarded up. They must have come up over Memorial Day to open it up. An empty house with unboarded windows seems vulnerable, more private. I am not tempted to look in. I am content with the strange sense of empowerment that comes with just being there, alone: I could look in those windows if I wanted to. I wouldn't be harming anyone or anything; and no one would know. In this brief moment I am queen of the island. It is my realm; and there is no one to refute the claim. I possess what I see.

But the houses, like sleeping princesses, will awake. Despite the frigid weather, it's supposed to be summer. A few houses, like my own, are already up and going. Still following the track along the shore, I emerge from the trees into the open fields of the village. The day is still grim and gray, but there is life here. I hear a boat entering the pool. Another arrival. Another opening.

Lost

We walk around Little Gotts Island at least once each summer. It's one of our rituals, repeated each year. And each
year is different. New blow-down creates new detours.
Fortunately, the Allen family, who own half the island, will
have cleared the path along the shore. And hopefully, the
lobster buoys will still be hanging on the trees at the edge
of the rocks to guide us to the place where we leave the
granite to begin the ascent toward the interior of the island.

Little Gotts is a different, and to this degree unknown, island. It is linked to Big Gotts at low tide; but with the incoming water, it retreats to its own self: separate, a small
world apart. No path goes to Little Gotts. The only route
by foot is the mussel bar, a strip of land that disappears for
hours of each day. Two family groups own the island, but
we know they are there only if we see a boat moored. On
Big Gotts we welcome visitors from Little Gotts like emis-
saries from a foreign country.

This year Chris joins us on the annual trek to Little Gotts.
As usual, the timing is crucial. We wait until the tide will
allow us to cross over the bar, complete the walk, and return to Big Gotts. We wear old sneakers to protect our feet
from the mussel shells and barnacles on the sharp stones of
the bar and carry our proper walking shoes. Once across,
we always sit on the same old driftwood log to change our
shoes. We leave the sneakers in the same spot, safe from
the tide.

We start by the Allens' cabin, stopping briefly to chat with
them if they happen to be in residence. Then we continue.

We know the way to the southern shore of the small island, a jumble of rocks. We jump the rocks. Happily the lobster buoy trail markers are securely in place. We find the spot where we leave the rocks and move inland, later to emerge on the shore again, this time further to the western side. The day is brilliant. We always choose a good day for the Little Gotts walk.

The path for many years has not followed the entire coastline of Little Gotts Island. At a certain point, from the western shore, we must turn into the interior, crossing the island to return to the shore where we have begun. It's a grassy spot. The way is easy here. We see the familiar foundation rectangle of a long-gone farmhouse; there's the old well where Lyford once tried, vainly, to access enough water to send by gravity feed down to the ever-thirsty Purcell cabin. A coil of black snaky pipe marked the spot. But we pass on, heading away from the sea.

Little Gotts is exactly that: a very small island. Soon we reach its center, the place of soft mosses underfoot, of dense trees and undergrowth. It is eerily silent. We do not hear the ocean or the sound of boats in the channel to the west. Although we have been here many times before, it always feels like unfamiliar territory. About a mile from home we are aliens in this place. We cannot read the landmarks; we can neither hear nor see the edge that would tell us we are even on an island. Every moss-covered hump of ground invites. None points out the way to go. I strike out to the right, but come only to a barrier thicket. John and Chris go directly left. No success there either. We have lost the path.

"But we have been here a zillion times," we protest to one another. "This is ridiculous." And rather embarrassing as well. Is it possible that we are lost? We stand in that mossy, ever dim place, the parents and the adult son. The parents can offer no guidance to the son, who in fact has been on this island as many times as we have. It is he who finally says he thinks he sees more of the sky at a point obliquely right.

"Wrong direction," I pronounce.

But I am wrong. We tramp on as Chris has suggested. The light grows brighter, we see still more of the sky, finally the edge of the island and the ocean beyond. But we're not where we thought we should be. We have emerged on the far side of the Allens' cabin.

"Let's hope they're not outside and we won't have to explain that we got lost and have come out in the wrong place," Chris says. Luck is with us. The Allens are inside. Chagrined, we creep past their cabin, finally reaching the shore and the still damp sneakers. There's time to put them on and make it back across the bar though the rising water is up to my knees by the time we reach Big Gotts.

Later, back home in Texas, Chris sends us a letter written on blue paper with white clouds. He recounts what he loved best about his week on the island with his wife and toddler son: "getting lost with my parents on a piece of land the size of a large city park."

A world we created each summer

Making the island ours

6

PROSPECTS

Near and Far

I was not expecting strange visions the day I saw an island looming. It was an ordinary day—the groceries just purchased at the Shop 'n' Save piled up in the boat, the hiss of beer cans being opened, the slow chugging of the motor on Russie Gott's old lobster boat, the Margaret Caroline. We were still in the channel but approaching Gotts Island when I saw it: an island I had never seen before, towering high, lightly shrouded in mist. It came suddenly upon us, stunning in its mystery.

"Looming," Russie said in his usual way. Short. To the point.

"*What's* looming?" I asked.

"No. *The* looming."

The real island I expected to see, Placentia, had disappeared. In its place arose a miasma, a hitherto unknown place. A new world.

It's a trick of the eye, a particular atmospheric phenomenon, we would tell ourselves later. But islands, perhaps more than other land formations, invite double looking. "The smaller and more enclosed [islands] are, the larger the window on the infinite, the farther they telescope into heaven," writes Philip Conkling. In the miniature we may see enormity, in the most particular detail, the universal.

I am not the only islander to have witnessed the looming. Ruth Moore saw it too, probably many times, and meditates upon the vision in "Time to Go—1930." The poem invites historical specificity: 1930 is the year of the final exodus from Gotts. But the island that is subject to time and change is juxtaposed to the poet's vision of those islands that loom up in the sea far to the westward:

> In the afternoon, the sea turned thunderous green,
> Clouds massed in the west.
> Near islands stood out big and clear; distant ones, through
> Some trick of the air,
> Lifted their ends out of water, as if the tide had tunneled
> Under them.

Nor is Moore alone in what she sees. She has an interlocutor. Though not named, he is clearly a fictionalized version of Montell Gott, uncle of Russie Gott and the last of the original community to live year-round on Gotts Island. It is he who announces simply, as Russie Gott would say to me, "The land looms." Exemplifying in his very loneness the exodus that lies in the distance of time, Uncle Mont says he has seen "them islands loom in wintertime like they was cut in two in the low places on'm. / Of a gray morning, cold, I seen them islands look like double-ender dories."

But on the real island, "Except for [Uncle Mont's] threshold, his tracks, no other footprints, / No boat but his, upended on the beach, / No fish-house but his opened and the banked crust scraped away." Vision, phantasma, and painful truth come together; the infinite looming, "mirage of islands," work of the imagination, contrasts with a more desolate reality that is subject to time. It is almost as if the emptiness of the island enables Moore and her companion to see the looming. The imaginary islands, unlike the real, are strangely immutable but visible only through the lens of a stark reality.

Tricks of the eye can tell us much about the realities of scale. How do we relate to the small—small islands, small objects? Why are we drawn to islands that appeared on medieval maps as much larger than they are, and are now represented as smaller and more remote?

To ensure the smallness of our islands we want to keep the dimensions intact. Boundedness is ostensibly essential to the larger, distant vision that we seek. "It is absolutely necessary that Lilliput be an island," writer Susan Stewart has observed. "The miniature world remains perfect . . . so long as its absolute boundaries are maintained." But Uncle Mont's Gotts Island is neither perfect nor ultimately bounded. It is, rather, a place that the old man looks out from. The island, the small, apparently finite container of loss, enables the view of the large. A there contains a not-there.

Loss sharpens the sight. In envisioning the looming, the two figures on the island see into what Rebecca Solnit calls the "blue of distance" that "comes with time, with the discovery of melancholy, of loss, of the texture of longing, of the complexity of the terrain we traverse, and of the years of travel." Seeing the distance is a function of memory. We have in memory what we cannot hold or literally see.

Seeing the distance comes with living, with "seeing" the long experience of time. The child's perception, in contrast, is limited to the close-up. When our grandchildren, Peter and Astrid, aged four and five, visited Gotts Island they had little interest in giant granite rocks or panoramic views out to sea; they paddled, like all children, in the pools nestled deep within the rocks, and attended to tiny stones, sea creatures, and shells. Theirs was the world of the small, the closely observed. In childhood there is no distance; all is foreground. Things stand simply for themselves and their place in the child's own world.

Only for the adult does the small thing, whether a formation of land in a sea or a personal object like the miniature portrait of the loved one contained in a locket, contain within it a special capacity to generate the absent, the distant, the lost. An eighteenth-century miniature portraitist in Charleston, South Carolina, called the miniature a "striking resemblance, that will never fail to . . . divert the cares of absence, and to aid affection in dwelling on those features and that image which death has forever wrested from us." The small is a presence that stands in for absence and expresses a relationship between the living and the dead.

But looking out from the small bounded island, we keep the distant where it is. Had I, or Ruth Moore, or Uncle Mont, been able to move closer to the islands we saw looming in the distance they would have dissolved into nothing. They belong to the distance. The key to seeing them is to have the place to look out from. The stone framed island is a window, a lens through which we view a larger space and, just as important, a larger span of time.

The small island always leads the eye outward: to the shore, the edge, the sea, and the horizon beyond. The large, un-wieldy but highly effective binoculars that John's father received as a retirement gift in 1962 have pride of place by our kitchen window. I use them daily. But what I see depends on what I know of the small piece of land on which I stand. And even if the magnification of the binoculars brings everything closer, I am still mindful that in Rebecca Solnit's remarkable phrase, "some things are not lost only so long as they are distant."

Small Worlds

The citizens of Maine's Monhegan Island saw much they didn't like in smallness. At issue was the proliferation of elf communities that left on the land footprints of no more than six to twelve inches. The diminutive structures built by children apparently became, for the adult islanders, the surrogates for larger, more diffuse threats: environmental, economic, demographic. In the fragility of the elf villages, the Monhegan islanders may have seen their own vulner-ability—and that of their island—to time, change, and loss. The adults, unlike the children, looked close but saw far. And displeased with what they saw, they stomped out the elves.

The elves came to Gotts Island too. I first saw their struc-tures in a patch of deep, lush mosses just to the side of the path that leads from our field to the old Strauss property. The children had built the tiny settlement in a secluded, protected spot that was once the edge of our pasture. The remnants of an old fence are still visible there, but now overwhelmed by the ever advancing, ever thickening, spruce. The builders had probably heard at least some of the island stories, the accounts of the village that was. Per-haps they had been told about the houses and barns, the school, the two churches, the shacks and sheds along the shore where the fishermen worked on nets and stored their gear. Perhaps they had even seen the old photograph of a group of island children rowing a dory at high water in the outer pool with the village houses on the hill in the back-ground. But whatever the children may or may not have thought or been told, their constructions were their own: houses, schools, farms, public meeting spaces—miniatures in stick and stone, an architecture of the fantastic and the mysterious.

A British anthropologist who visited us that summer crawled around on his knees to take photographs of the miniature structures. He wanted more information. "The children built them," was all we could tell him. It didn't seem to matter that we didn't know which children. Better not to know, to savor the mystery. I could easily have figured out that the children of the Baldwin family were the likely suspects—not very many children live on the island, and one always knows who is there—but the fact is, I didn't want to pursue the matter.

And sooner or later, more miniature houses, stunning in their intricacy, began to appear that summer, especially in the woods along the southern edge of the town road.

But I wasn't thinking of the elf house builders that day when I went out in my red running shorts to jog down the town road, carefully picking my way among the inevitable roots. I had just entered the woods, just passed the place where the sunny fields of the old village give way, in striking transition, to the darkness of the spruce. This is my favorite point on the town road, and on this particularly warm day, the woods were cool, shady, and welcoming, the ground soft beneath my feet.

I rarely see anyone there. Coming upon the oldest Baldwin child, standing in the middle of the path, striking a kind of ballet pose, arms akimbo the way that eleven year old girls do, was a surprise. The girl didn't expect to be seen. She was just taking a few moments off from her labors while her younger brother and sister, further along the path, still knelt in the soft soil, working to perfect their tiny houses. Perhaps she felt the need to stand and stretch after all that work on all fours, to reach out and grasp the stillness of the woods.

But I felt the encounter as an invasion on my part, an occasion of embarrassment for us both. It wasn't only that I had found out the elf builders, that I had happened upon knowledge not intended to be known, and had learned a fact that would destroy the somehow essential mystery; nor was it just that the destruction of the mystery would also change the woods, render them more ordinary simply because more known. It wasn't only that, though that was large in itself. Rather it was that the girl thought she was alone to embrace the beauty of the woods and mosses. I had interrupted an important moment that in its way defined childhood itself; and in so doing I had also inadvertently reminded her that the moments of childhood will, after all, come to an end. Some middle-aged woman in red shorts will come along and break into the child's world, impose another scale upon it.

I was the awkward Gulliver among the inhabitants of Lilliput. For me, the scale was out of joint. Later, when our anthropologist friend showed us the photographs he had taken of the elf structures it was impossible to tell that they were a mere six inches high. Only the shot with a human hand interposed within it would tell the tale. Without the hand, small and large, near and far, folded into each other. We could not tell if we were looking at a six-inch rock or a high cliff, a puddle or a veritable ocean.

The island contains them all, the elf villages and tiny lichens of the woodsy interior, and the granite boundaries that in both physical size and geological history spell enormity. Time encodes itself in both the small and the large. The island juxtaposes the minute and the gigantic, intensifying, even confusing, the scale of things. We, like Gulliver, may escape Lilliput but then find ourselves in the land of the Brobdingnagians, where, as elves among the giants, we must seek to know our human place.

The span of human habitation on the island, the small history mimicked in the children's elf houses, is minute by comparison with the enormity of geological time. Stone is its given. The rocks, Ruth Moore wrote, "say how old is old." The granite speaks of great eruptive volcanoes pushed up to the earth's surface by the force of increasing quantities of molten rock. The rocks contain the story of the long period when the present coast of Maine was turned into a great cauldron of fire.

How easily we conflate history in a paragraph, the history of the earth's substance, the history of human settlement, depopulation and disappearance. A small, sinuous crenellation in the rock, Philip Conkling reminds us, gives evidence of a "continental collision." A small outcrop yields evidence of an enormously dramatic, even catastrophic, history. The scale of the event cannot be contained in its mark; language becomes understatement, even irony. We want to return to the human scale. It's the human hand in the photograph that gives us confidence and security, sets our world straight after all.

I know who they were, the original islanders, the names listed in H.W. Small's *History*, inscribed on the cemetery stones, and recorded—albeit rather idiosyncratically by first names—in Philip Moore's account books now piled up in the upstairs back bedroom of our house. But viewed in the long lens of historical time and against the hugeness of the natural environment, known only through name or occasional anecdote, the human scale shrinks to the smallest dimension. Mindful of both temporal and spatial enormity, I walk among the people of the island's past, searching for perspective; but memory and imagination collide.

Perhaps, then, the island children, for whom the here and now is the essential element, get it right. The builders of the elf houses are content in their worlds of the little. The children I interrupted as they built tiny structures on the town road did not return the next summer. But I wished that they had come back. I wanted them to see for themselves that, miraculously, the miniature world they had created was largely intact. The elf houses, these tiny, apparently frail structures, constructed of sticks, lichens, seeds, and diminutive pebbles, had withstood the Maine winter and were still there. Some force, some natural circumstance, had kept the small structures safe amidst the mosses while less than half a mile away the winter winds and seas thundered and beat against the great granite slabs that mark the island's bounds.

Strange Beings

What is distant is not only in a sense more real; it may also be strange. On a good day, when I look out from my Gotts Island house to forty miles of coast, ocean, and islands, Placentia Island is my special marker. It is the largest island I can see in any detail: its ring of rock, massed thickness of spruce, short stretch of stony beach. There it lies, out beyond the white rectangle of the Gotts Island cemetery and the town road.

I see my neighbors going along the road, pushing their carts and wheelbarrows on their way to, or returning from, the dock. This is my home, these are the people I know. But Placentia Island, once named Plaisance, the place of pleasure, is just beyond the limit of the known. I can name it, I can name the Kellams, the couple who lived alone there for almost fifty years; but even with binoculars, in all those years that the Kellams were there, their dory, pulled up on the stretch of beach, was the only sign of the human I could ever see on that island.

Sarah Orne Jewett once wrote of the "strange beings" who inhabited the coast of Maine, clinging to "isolated bits of the world." Jewett and others have taught us a sensitivity to oddness, people we cannot understand in the usual way and who, precisely for that reason, draw us to their stories. The Kellams would have been grist for Jewett's mill. They were a mystery. They were not Maine natives, but neither were they summer people like us. They belonged to their own category, living by themselves, summer and winter, on their island. When Mr. Kellam died, by then in his seventies, the local fishermen are said to have told his wife that they couldn't be responsible for her living out there by herself all winter. She had been forced to leave her island and move to the mainland, where she died several years later.

Whatever we knew about the Kellams, they remained, like Gotts Island's Miss Peterson, essentially unknown, never to be known. But with their island, Placentia, there before me, so near and yet so far, the reclusive couple were for decades always a presence. And I, like those narrators in Jewett's fictions, was the distanced viewer. In all those years, I never once set foot on Placentia Island. Each island is like a world in itself. I felt that Placentia was off-limits. Like islands that loom, I needed to keep Placentia in the distance, the Kellams, a mysterious given. To have actually met them might have destroyed the imaginative power they generated. I preferred to surmise, not to ask questions for which there were no real answers.

THE KELLAMS

"Well, it was not my idea of the Kellams."

We were speaking in Berkeley, California, Carl, my Gotts Island neighbor, and I. Gotts Island, Placentia Island, summertime in coastal Maine were far away. But we'd all seen the article on the Kellams in the *New York Times*. It marked the publication of the catalogue for an exhibit of photographs of Placentia Island and its late inhabitants. Carl had already read the catalogue. We were still awaiting our copy from Amazon.com.

The *Times* article came out the day before Valentine's Day. It was a love story. The Kellams, the hermit couple on Placentia Island, were billed as the epitome of the loving duo, even leaving each other *billets doux* that marked particular spots in their island paradise.

Well, maybe. But we are talking about an island in Maine, not Tahiti. There is still the enormity of it all. Yes, that's the issue. They lived on Placentia Island, just the two of them, for almost fifty years. The *Times* writer seemed to have such little awareness of what that actually means.

But think: an island in Maine in winter, an island with no contact with the mainland. Long dark nights, howling winds, bitter cold, isolation. They ate canned food and stayed up on winter nights to feed small logs into a stove that would not take larger ones. If the stove had gone out, they could have frozen to death.

"A couple's love created their world," the caption of one of the photographs reads. The images are evocative and beautiful. They are also taken in the summer.

One cannot get round the question of motivation: Was Mr. Kellam involved in the Manhattan Project? Or, was he, as my Gotts Island neighbors who knew him and his wife think, simply looking for a purer life? "The answer is only in their hearts," a commentator from the Nature Conservancy is quoted as having remarked.

The inadequacy of language astounds. But my discomfort is more complicated than that. It's not just that the *Times* writer gets some of the facts wrong, that the Maine his informants describe is not the one I know. No, it's more even than this. It's that the pages of the newspaper freeze the Kellams, endow them with an identity, imply concrete knowledge. The hermit couple have been made in some way understandable to people reading the *New York Times* on the day before Valentine's Day.

The Kellams may well exemplify a particular loving relationship, but its representation in the newspaper seems offensive. Something has been breached, something that needs to remain in mystery. Yes, mystery. That's the way it is on the offshore islands, the way of all the stories. It's the very lack of concreteness that counts.

I think that's what Carl meant. He wanted his idea, unsubstantiated or even inaccurate, of the Kellams. And I wanted mine. I want the Kellams whom I never saw on their island but could imagine as I peered out from my high kitchen window on Gotts; the Kellams whose real story will simply never be known.

STORM

The wind blows hard out of the northeast today. A lead-gray sky threatens rain. All day long we've fed the fire in the stove. I hear the repeated thwack as John loads up logs in the old wood box.

I'm standing at the kitchen window watching the waves smash white on Placentia Island far across the bay. Now that the Kellams have gone, no one lives there of course. Just several days ago the neighbors said that since the Nature Conservancy has taken over control of the island, even the meager 'improvements' to the Kellams' old cabin have been removed. The Conservancy people don't want visitors camping out there.

I learned this the day that we were all having drinks at the Weinbergs' house—Northwood and Rita Kenway, John and I; and with the second round, the shadows lengthening in the field behind the garden and shed, the talk had turned to the Kellams and their lives on Placentia.

"He thought the world was corrupting, you know; and the only thing a good person could do was renounce it. So they came to Maine and bought Placentia Island, all 750 acres, for $10,000." This was Northwood's contribution, new intelligence to me, but it seemed plausible that anyone who elected in early middle age to spend the rest of his life on an island, with only his wife for company, must have some philosophy like that. I just hadn't heard it articulated before.

"What about his wife, what did *she* think?" I wanted to ask. I would save that one up for later. The conversation had moved to renunciation, escape: "And how can one really 'escape' the world?" I asked instead. I was thinking of investments, groceries, mail—practical matters like that.

Northwood agreed. "O yes. They had to pay taxes, buy postage stamps, to say nothing of the canned goods they lived on."

How long, I mused, did their letters sit on a table or windowsill in the cabin at Placentia Island, awaiting the sporadic trips in the dory to the mainland and the post office?

But now everyone wanted to talk about Mrs. Kellam, Nan. I had always thought of that isolated pair as Mr. and Mrs. Kellam. But to the Weinbergs and the Kenways, they were "Art and Nan." Odd that I had never thought of them with first names. At any rate, the topic was now Nan.

Northwood and Rita Kenway had spent their honeymoon on Gotts Island in August 1950, and in neighborly fashion had rowed over to Placentia to visit the Kellams, who had been living there about a year. Rita remembered well the visit they had made as a newly married couple; she recalled the pleasure the Kellams had expressed in welcoming their surprise guests. "They weren't hermits, you know," she said.

Years later, the Kellams became the godparents of Nancy, the Kenways' fourth and last child. There they are in a photograph of the baptismal party at Gotts Island, Rita holding the baby Nancy in her arms, the others looking on admiringly. That was about 1961. And many more years after that, when Nancy graduated from college, the Kellams sent her a generous check.

So the Kenways had remained friends with the reclusive couple, right up until the end. After Art died, Northwood went over to Placentia to set up a solar lighting system for Nan. He had done a good job of it, was sorry that the Conservancy had now dismantled everything.

"She needed the solar system," Northwood was explaining, "because she had never learned to light the Aladdin kerosene lamps. She couldn't even change the batteries in a flashlight."

"Couldn't change flashlight batteries?" That was my question.

"No, " Northwood repeated. And when Art had the stroke that was to kill him three days later, Nan had to hail down the Swans Island ferry—it must have been a Thursday or a Sunday because the ferry went to Long Island, and hence close to Placentia, only on those days—anyway, she had to hail down the ferry, shouting from the beach that is close to the channel, because she couldn't figure out how to insert the battery into the ship-to-shore phone. Or rather, she didn't know that the phone *required* the battery that was still nestling in its case.

"She lived for almost fifty years on an island with no electricity and couldn't light an Aladdin lamp or insert batteries in a flashlight or a phone"?

"No. Art always did it."

Now it was Michael Weinberg's turn. He too remembered the day when Nan had tried unsuccessfully to use the phone and then, just as unsuccessfully, to raise the "need help" flag on the flagpole (since she and Art had never needed help, the flagpole mechanism was too rusty to function). It was the day that Michael's sons, Andy and Ben, launched the peapod they had built in the attic.

Perhaps I mis-heard this. Why would the Weinberg sons build a boat in the *attic*? But Michael was already explaining how the boys had removed a window and part of a wall and had constructed a kind of sling to hoist the boat down from the attic—which must have been an odd sight: two boys launching a boat from an attic. Anyway, the story was that the boys ultimately got the boat out and hauled it down to the pool; and they launched their boat and set off on its maiden voyage, a row to Placentia, on the very day that Nan hailed down the ferry. They noticed that the Swans Island ferry, on its way that day to Long Island, had stopped near Placentia, and they saw Nan Kellam on the shore shouting. So they rowed in and, with the strength required to haul a peapod out of an attic, they now helped to hoist Art from the cabin down to the shore. And someone must have called the Coast Guard because Art did get to the hospital in Bar Harbor. But he died not long after his arrival there.

So that left Nan, who couldn't change a flashlight battery, alone on Placentia Island. It was unthinkable that she spend a winter there, but she could manage the warmer months, and people pitched in to help. That's how Ben Weinberg happened to go out to the island to cut wood. Nan showed Ben the exact size that the wood would have to be cut, the size that would fit in their stove. That stove, with its small capacity, was of course famous on the island. Ben certainly didn't need to be instructed about the size of the logs.

"Just show me where you want me to cut the wood," he had said to Nan Kellam. "Where is the wood lot?"

"I don't know," Nan had replied. "Art always did it."

CR

The rain has come. In gusts and sheets it blows against the east windows and scuds across the fields. The fire spits and crackles in the stove behind me. With the tide out, the waves boil against the exposed ledges in the outer pool, and I watch them beat white against the rocky shore of far-off Placentia. Did Nan, after she had moved to the mainland, think of the island, of putting the small logs into the stove on a raging winter night, of rowing in the dory to deliver her letters to the post office, and finally, of rushing down to the shore to hail the ferry because she can't get the phone to work without batteries?

The wild afternoon wears on. John and I are now drinking single malt scotch and talking about the Kellams again. We're talking about people on islands, about reclusives. We expect something of them after all, something extraordinary: some special will, heroic quality, obsession, self-reliance, or even insight. But the picture is out of joint. Nan couldn't change the batteries in the flashlight. She didn't know where the wood lot was. She just followed Art. What are we to think of this, of the ordinary I mean? Why are our expectations so disappointed? I wanted Nan to be different, stronger. Could any woman just follow her husband to fifty years of isolation on Placentia Island? Surely all those years of living as a solitary couple on an island, with little or no communication with the mainland, took more than that.

But what was it?

The gale has set in even stronger. The natural light is almost gone in my warm kitchen. Placentia Island fades into gray-dark mist.

LIGHT

"There's a light on Placench." John was standing in the kitchen peering out into the black night. Except for a few solar-powered bulbs carefully husbanded by their owners, Gotts Island is a place without electricity. The night is dark indeed, a light always noticed.

But John had to be wrong. There are no lights on Placentia Island. And even when the Kellams were still there, no light from their woods-bound house could be seen from Gotts.

I saw the Kellams only once, on a glorious day in July, around 1979 or 1980, when they came over to Gotts Island to visit the Kenways. It was perfect weather for taking out the rowing dory, and a day when the tide was high at noon in the Gotts Island pool. From the upstairs bedroom window that looks west I watched the dory make its way slowly and deliberately across the bay. I knew it had to be the Kellams.

I can't see the Gotts Island dock from my house, but I knew I would catch sight of the visitors from Placentia when they came up the path toward the Kenways' house. There's only one route to the Kenways' door. I would see the Kellams, just as I see everyone, coming round the curve by the rose bushes. I only had to wait by my window.

So I waited, wondering what they would look like, this couple who lived alone, all year round, on Placentia Island. But I had not thought about time, about how, like the formidable winters on Placench, the years might have frozen the Kellams. Nor had I thought about fashion as the gauge of time. But here, coming up the Kenways' path, was a woman wearing a 1950s skirt, "anklets," and saddle oxfords. I hadn't seen saddle oxfords—or anklets—in more than twenty-five years. She must have brought them with her when she and her husband left California in 1949 to move to the island they had purchased in Maine. They must have survived all those summers and winters in closet or chest. Mrs. Kellam, a woman who had at that time lived with her husband for some thirty years on an island in Maine, their only contact with the mainland that rowing dory, was a person from another age.

The visitor in saddle shoes came from an island that the French navigators once called Grande Plaisance (which distinguished it from Gotts or Petite Plaisance). Even translated literally into English as "Great Pleasure," the name comes from another world. Perhaps just as well that Grande Plaisance became Placentia and finally, in the voices of the local people, Placench. It's as if the folly of a French queen acquired a nasal New England diminutive and thus became the suitable home of a reclusive couple from California. They had come to create their own version of pleasure.

"What's Placentia like"? I once asked Russie Gott.

"Just trees," he said.

The Kellams were newcomers in Russie's scheme of things, people from "away." Their presence didn't really count for much. Certainly not in any way he would discuss with me. He knew I was not asking about the topography or the flora and fauna of Placentia Island. He knew I wanted to know about the Kellams. Russie had a lot of answers but was dismissive of some questions. I had asked the wrong one.

And yet I remember the question and I clearly remember when I asked it. It was the day that I saw the looming. Later that would seem a coincidence: I wanted an explanation of the real place, and I was given an apparition: the looming, mirage of the sea. Placench, so solid in its greenness, presided over by a woman in saddle oxfords, disappeared. In its place arose a magic isle—*grande plaisance*, a place of wondrous pleasures—high and shimmering. From this new island one might just hope to see, emerging from the mists, the fairy proprietors, Mr. and Mrs. Kellam, rowing their double-ended bark.

But magic moments come only once. Mirages quickly pass. Russie Gott has been dead for more than ten years, and the

Kellams are gone. The light we saw, a trick of the eye, had a clear explanation. It wasn't on Placentia Island at all. I was right about that. We were looking at the mast light on a sloop tied up for the night on Russie's old mooring off the tip of Little Gotts Island. A real family, from Camden, Rockport, or Northeast Harbor, slept beneath that light. And as their boat swayed with the movement of the tide, they probably did not even know that they were moored in a channel of the imagination with a fairy island just off the port side.

Fog

Finally, after days of hot sun rare on the island, came the fog and the damp, turning the berrying patches wet and oozy, plumping almost instantly the wizening blueberries, bringing out a pungent aroma in the juniper and bayberry. I'm watching a figure move against the complex geometries of the cemetery fence. The figure is rounded, head down, shoulders sloping, heading along the path toward Harriet's house. I can't tell who it is. All is mystery, all obscure, in the fog. Figures make entrances and exits on a stage backed with white gauze.

John Clark's trees by the shore of the inner pool have grown so tall that they appear as a great bulbous form rising above the hillside like clouds in a Turner landscape. But there is no color here today. Only gray and white. The trees are my marker of both time and weather: How much can I see of them? How much not? How much have they grown since last year?

John Clark has agreed to allow Northwood to cut down his trees, which in their height and thickness are obscuring Northwood's view. It's no small task for anyone, particularly for a man in his mid-seventies. Each day, Northwood tells me, he takes down another tree. I hear the chain saw. Relentless. When I pass the spot on the way to the dock, I see the growing pile of brush, neatly assembled by the path. A massive woodpile grows ever larger. I wonder what Northwood will do with all that wood. There must be sixty large trees down there. How many wood fires would that be?

In the still dense fog the chain saw whirrs on. I hate the noise, but each tree that comes down opens up my view as well. When they are all gone, we will be able to see once again the Green Head and, at low tide, the bar to Little Gotts. The broad vista from my high windows will be restored.

But I will not see that great soft shape on foggy days.

The morning progresses. Image and sound come clearer. The cloud that marks the remaining clump of John Clark's trees turns into a distinct outline, each doomed tree still standing visible on its own. I can now tell what is near and what is far; I am back in touch with the scale of things. The detail on the cemetery fence comes gradually into view, no longer a mere vague line of white, hardly distinguishable in a gray-white world.

7

STONE

The cemetery marks the place and time: a birth in Princeton, New Jersey, 1965, a death at the Masai Mara, Kenya, 1991. The message in stone is cryptic, no weeping willows and curvaceous angels. The dates simply bookend a life, leaving all else to us the living.

Ben has joined the other island dead, all in their rightful place. The official deed conveying the land for the Gotts Island cemetery is dated 1875; but the oldest stone with a date is that of one Susanna Thurstin who died in 1811. Whether officially designated or not, a place to house the dead had to be designated by the newly founded village. An official deed was not required. It could come later.

These early Gotts Island planners—though no doubt acting more from necessity than plan—chose a space central to the community that would emerge and develop. It is important to keep the dead in their place, historian Gary Laderman has pointed out, to create a permanent dwelling place for them. But their place, the island cemetery, is also our place. The gates, after all, have been removed from the eastward facing fence. We move in and out of this cemetery. Death itself is not buried here. Perhaps paradoxically, the cemetery, like the island, actually delineates a circle of the living. The task is to engage in a continuing re-animation of that circle.

ℭℛ

Memory is often kind, tending to obliterate the pain of our worst moments of loss. Such memories are fragmentary: the phone call at 2 a.m., the conversation with Ben's friend Michelle.

Michelle: "There's been an accident."

Tina: "Is he living?"

Michelle: "No."

It was already late morning in Kenya. Because this death has occurred in another time and place it seems at first less real. Yet we want to name the moment of the event. It marks the boundary after which everything will be different.

We had spoken with him on Christmas morning, Berkeley time. He told us he would be flying the next morning, Kenyan time. He told us he had just had some minor surgery on a precancerous patch on his face. I wondered if he would have a scar, slightly worried that he would suffer some small mark. Interesting now that I remember that concern, that small mark. He would still have had the wound when he died.

In the living room was the DHL box with the gifts that he had sent: African statuettes, a belt, all still in their box and packed away in our closet. John's mother was with us for the holiday; there were gifts for her as well.

John came into the kitchen. I think I was still on the phone with Michelle, but I cannot remember that. I believe it was I who told John. We then went into the guest room to tell Ruth, John's mother, who was not asleep. She had heard the voices in the kitchen, perhaps even had heard the phone ring. She was a person of few words. We told her the news. She said nothing, lay still in the bed. We would later remember that stillness, and John, in the pain of his own grief, would be disappointed and angry; and then, as she neared her own death two years later at age ninety, we would learn to put it all in another frame. We would know how much she loved both of her grandsons, and that she simply could not articulate her shock.

Chris was in California also that Christmas holiday, but had spent Christmas Day and night with a friend somewhere near Calistoga. We had no contact information for the place. We only knew he was coming back on the 26th. All that morning, as we kept going over and over the news in our own minds, we imagined him doing whatever he was doing, unaware that a boundary had been passed and that his brother was dead. We were living in a rented house on Grizzly Peak, at the top of the Berkeley hills. I knew that Chris would walk up the hill from the BART station. It was a matter of watching out for him. Finally I saw him come round the corner, cross the street, head for the house. I remember his jaunty walk. It was the walk of someone who has not heard the news that would make the difference. John and I met him at the door. And then his world fell out of focus just as ours had done.

The following days began to flow into one another. There were the conversations with the embassy in Kenya, the realization that the bodies in the plane were burned beyond simple visual identification, the phone call to the orthodontist in New Jersey who had straightened Ben's teeth

thirteen years earlier and had full mouth x-rays. The orthodontist was kind enough to make a special trip down
to his x-ray archive, get the pictures, and send them to the
address we gave him in Africa.

Since Michelle, her mother, and Ben's yellow lab, Beja, were
coming home and would land in Philadelphia on January 5,
bringing Ben's ashes with them, John, Chris, Ruth, and I
made plans to fly east. We arrived at Newark on a bitterly
cold night. I remember that the rented car had just, stu-
pidly, been washed and was instantly covered in a cocoon
of ice. We couldn't get into it, let alone drive it. The agency
had to find another car. Finally, a sad and miserable group,
we bundled ourselves into the second car and set off on the
drive down to our Princeton house. From there, the next
day, we would drive to Philadelphia, meet Michelle, and
receive from her the box of Ben's ashes. It was the beginning of a process that would culminate, six months later, in
a simple burial in the Gotts Island cemetery.

These are the "facts" as I remember them; and they are important as far as they go. But I now see them as if in the
reverse end of a telescope: distanced, almost unreal, like
looking out to sea from the island on a foggy day. They do
not tell the story I want to tell. They only motivate the story. They describe the loss in only one way; the real subject
here is the way in which we incorporate the dead into our
own circle, our own place, our own language. We make
them ours in the memories we hold, the stories we tell.
The so-called facts remain secondary to the process.

The ritual is never totally complete. Boundaries are not
that real. And I am thankful for that. Why must we accept a
strict border between the living and the dead? Several years

ago, at a conference I organized at Berkeley titled "Seeing the Difference," poet and critic Sandra Gilbert movingly described viewing the body of her husband, Eliot, and becoming suddenly aware of the "plausibility" of death: "I realize that such a feeling must account for traditional images of dead people 'living' as it were, on 'the other side' of a sometimes permeable, at least semi-transparent barrier . . . When one 'goes,' one goes somewhere. Somewhere plausible." For me, now that more than a decade has passed since Ben's death, the boundary is still in some sense permeable or porous, still open like the fence in the island cemetery.

Ruth Moore's chatty, amiable Phebe Bunker seems to have little difficulty in making her way back to the island years after her death. In the island cemetery the dead have a place to return to, and we have a place in which to remember them. Phebe tells a story about time, change, and the ways that a community of the past connects with the present. She reminds us that the dead, and the land they inhabited, are still with us, the living. Memory makes place. Place makes memory.

That's the point of the famous tale of the banquet attended by the poet Simonides of Ceos. According to the story, while Simonides is out of the banqueting hall, the roof crashes down, crushing to death the host and all the other guests. The bodies are so mangled that the survivors cannot identify their relatives to take them away for burial. But luckily, Simonides remembers the places at which everyone had been sitting at the table, and he is able to say who is who among the bodies. In short, spatial arrangement is an essential part of the memory process.

Gotts Island has its own Simonides. In her book on the island inhabitants, Rita Kenway gives us an organized list of stones and names in the island cemetery. I know the names because I know where they now belong; and even more important, though undoubtedly now changed over time, I know the places they walked. The island, sitting on its foundation of stone, is a house of memory in which we associate, and remember, certain images or experiences because they are connected with particular places. And within its geography, defined both physically and emotionally, the cemetery is the central space, the location to which all others relate.

Sites and spaces, and the relationships among them, give us a language for absence and loss. But we speak too through imagining wholes in parts, through substitutions and surrogates. One story substitutes for another. An empty foundation stands in for the unknown and the absent. A story of illness and loss recorded in a diary in 1852 derives its power from the constancy of the wind. A neighbor whose son is buried in the cemetery bestows loving care on maintaining the cemetery ground. We ourselves choose a cemetery plot for its proximity to our son, as if this will bring separation to an end.

It's all about making, doing, substituting, connecting, remembering. It's about building something that will at least appear to be a whole. Never mind the missing parts. They will take care of themselves.

Foundation

That summer of 1964, feeling new to the island, we didn't particularly notice the old foundation behind our house. It was the summer we rented the "box on the rocks," the small cottage that sat squat on the ledges at the furthest eastern edge of the land. From our little house we didn't look back toward the rectangle of stone and the path that led to the village a mile away. The sea, pounding the granite just yards in front of us, was so much more compelling. We knew, only in the way that one knows certain facts, that the foundation stones, blocks of pink granite now marked with yellow-gold lichens, were all that remained of Miss Peterson's house. The fire, in the winter of 1926, had taken everything else.

The story of Miss Peterson's death in that fire was already old in 1964. The foundation, an empty granite rectangle, one of several on the island, had become a quiet ghost sharing with us a border between the land and the sea, known and unknown. Not recognizing that margin, we didn't ask the ghost to speak. No one knows exactly how Miss Peterson came to die that wintry night. We surmise: perhaps a stroke or a heart attack and a fatal fall while holding a lantern. It seems plausible. It suffices. It's all we can know. This is the way of all such deaths, all accidents.

"My son was killed by a bird," I might say if asked about Ben's death. But the statement, startling and unreal, is inadequate, even foreign, to the freight it bears. The event belongs to a place that imagination cannot penetrate. With no real story, we have only an outline, a trace that stands strangely alone.

So I return, years later, to Miss Peterson's story. It is my surrogate story, similarly incomplete; and I am drawn to it despite the danger that it will take over. If I can grasp, even fabricate, some of that story, I think, then I might achieve some control over the one I really want to be able to tell and to know.

Miss Peterson's story belongs to this place that I know. It's a Maine story, an island narrative, supposedly contained like the speck of rockbound land that is the island itself. Envisioning the fire that enveloped Miss Peterson's house by the granite ledges at Gotts Island, I see the flames rising from a ruined plane in a perpetually grassy place thousands of miles away.

There is no stone in that African plain, no granite to mark the spot. I know that place only in the photographs I took there as a tourist two years before Ben's death. The island—Miss Peterson's island, our island—is the place of stone markers that are at least partially readable. Perhaps that's why it seemed so right to bring the ashes of our son from a savannah in Africa to a white-fenced cemetery on an island bounded by stone.

The grave, the cemetery, the island are all bounded. They contain memory, they are the vessels of stories, they connect stories. But anyone who speaks of the "tyranny of completeness" on islands is wrong: even here, we can only attempt completion. An accident report, a newspaper feature, a novel—all are partial stories, spaces defined by the structure of a narrative whose real content remains an emptiness. Ben's death taught me that knowing means filling in as best one can, accepting truth in fragments. The foundation stones that mark the remains of Miss Peterson's

Keeping watch

Signs of emptiness, traces of the past

house do not speak after all. Whatever voice they have must
be ours.

CR

But these thoughts were to come only years later. That first
summer we had other things on our minds. John was draft-
ing his Ph.D. dissertation; I was occupied with the enormity of the sea, the danger it posed to the then fourteen-
month-old Chris, the challenge of transporting a summer's
worth of books and groceries by wheelbarrow down a mile
of rut-riven path. When the fogs of early summer finally
cleared, I hung Chris's diapers out near the granite blocks
that marked the foundation wall. I saw the low wall as simply a demarcation between the human space and the huge
natural ledges adjacent to it. There was a kind of safety in
that wall, but I did not then imagine the house or the woman who had inhabited it.

It was the next year, now expecting Ben, that we bought the
old Moore family house in the remains of the village on the
western side of the island. We left the "box on the rocks"
to other renters, and ultimately a new owner, who added
a pitched roof that rendered that house no longer a box.
Other people's laundry would be hung to dry near Miss
Peterson's foundation. Our family, ultimately four, became
part of the old village, removed from the ledges, salt spray,
and pounding sea. We took a route that Miss Elizabeth Peterson, more than seventy years earlier, had renounced.

Perhaps Miss Peterson's story, her decision to build her
house at the far eastern point of the island, is about renunciation. But what, then, was renounced? Questions like
this beg answers, motivate other people's stories. Ruth

Moore had written about Miss Peterson's decision in her 1950s novel, *Speak to the Winds*. So had Ted Holmes, who remembers going to parties Miss Peterson held for the island children. That was long before Ted grew up to become the professor of English at the University of Maine who taught writing to Stephen King, Maine's master of gothic.

Perhaps she was a recluse, perhaps because of some physical deformity she wished to live beyond the village ("she was very ugly" one report says); or perhaps, as Moore surmises in her novel, Miss Peterson simply wanted to see "the sea [spread out] from rocks to sky." Her decision may have been not so much a renunciation of the village as a seeking of space for herself.

Ruth and Ted, local chroniclers of the island, were probably better informed than Katherine Crosby, who had arrived with such confidence and authority, more than two decades earlier to investigate Miss Peterson's story. Crosby hadn't known that she would reach an edge, a boundary of the known. But I know the path she took and the slightly rising curve that brings Miss Peterson's site suddenly into view. I see the writer, perhaps with her notebook already containing the comments she has heard from the village women, coming around that curve, past the place where the lichens and upland cranberries now cling to mossy rock. She has made this trip, probably from Boston to Bar Harbor, she has hired a boatman, climbed the hill to the village, walked out to the easternmost point of the island—only to discover a story contained, silently, in an empty foundation and the ruined remnant of a chimney.

I imagine all of this. Perhaps Crosby took another way to Miss Peterson's house, approached it not by the direct route

through the center of the island but by the path that follows
the curve of the shore at southern neck cove. Let me return to what I know. Miss Peterson's house was certainly
real. I mean real in the sense of walls, a roof (gambrel),
windows, a garden. There's even a photograph of the house
on the back cover of *Speak to the Winds*. But in the book
jacket photograph, Miss Peterson's house, gray and strong
as it is, looks oddly out of place in its rocky setting by the
sea. It looks like a house that should have been built on any
street, in any normal town of the period. It would have
been more appropriate if built in the village on the west
side of the island, even though its curved roof line would
have been at odds with the sharply angled mid-nineteenth-
century houses that cluster around the white rectangle of
the cemetery.

The what-was and what-is do not seem to fit. The house is
an anomaly, remote, like history that cannot be recreated.
The foundation is the real now. As the years after Ben's
death marched by, I was drawn increasingly to those stony
imprints that are the markers of depopulated places like
the Maine offshore islands, signifiers of emptiness that exert their own particular force, drawing us in and defying
explanation all at the same time. It's as if these stone footprints were meant to stand alone, meant to continue long
after wood and beam have burned, rotted, or fallen under
the weight of winter snow.

Empty foundations delineate in striking relief the story of
transformation, of ending. Miss Peterson's death in the fire
at Gotts Island belongs to that very time when the island
was undergoing the process of depopulation and desertion
whose compelling markers we live with now. We come

upon them in unexpected places: in glades, fields, and forest. A new break in the woods will reveal a wall we have not
seen before. We follow the stones, become enmeshed in a
hopeless thicket, retreat to the open field by the sea. The
square foundation is so at odds with the irregular boundaries of the island itself, the granite slabs that seem so ageless,
so resistant to change. Turning the imagination inward, the
sparse stony traces of houses long gone serve not so much
aesthetic as need. The foundation of Miss Peterson's house
renders the actual house less concrete, even when I have
seen its photograph, when I have read a diary account by a
man who had tea with Miss Peterson there, when I know
that a real house burned to the ground, its owner perishing
in the flames.

But the foundation markers, even if partially filled now
with straggly spruce or summer grasses, remain essentially
empty and unyielding. What do I know of an event that took
place at the edge of the granite rocks at Gotts Island almost
eighty years ago, or of one that occurred on Christmas Day
on a grassy plain in Africa half-way around the world? I have
only the sparse details of an accident report for the latter.
I know the plane left Mombassa on schedule that morning,
on its regular trip to a game park lodge in the interior. I
know it is not uncommon for vulture-like birds to be in the
vicinity of the park lodges.

But where do accident stories begin? Which facts are rel-
evant? I know that Miss Peterson's route to the house at
Gotts Island began in Philadelphia, where her family had
been well established from early in the nineteenth century.
I discover in the *Dictionary of National Biography* that the Pe-
tersons were a publishing family, producing *Peterson's Maga-*

zine, which in 1864 was the largest-selling ladies magazine in North America, as well as the *Saturday Evening Post*. I look up *Peterson's Magazine* on microfilm for the years 1870–1900; I find essays and fictions that seem strangely at odds with the image of a lone woman pushing a wheelbarrow to a solitary house by the sea.

I begin to see Miss Peterson as a woman of the margin, this summer person from the Philadelphia suburb of Lansdowne who, to the wonder of everyone, built her house on the granite rock far from the village, and then, in just as startling a manner, chose to remain all year round in that house. The year came when Miss Peterson did not return to Lansdowne at the end of the summer. With that defining moment, Miss Peterson achieved a status for which there was no name.

Even if I accept the incomplete, I want to name things, to put people and places in categories. Stories are supposed to have facts. There were only two categories of persons on Gotts Island: local people whose families had been there through the nineteenth century, and summer people. Miss Peterson came as a summer person and then fell into a category of her own. She founded an Episcopal church on the island; and surely aware of those sixth-century followers of St. Columba's ministry centered on the Scottish island of Iona, those monks whose lives were defined by the isolation of rocky eruptions, cells, caves, and lands barren of vegetation, surely aware of those connections with salt and rock, she named her church St. Columba's.

The first service at St. Columba's Episcopal Mission Church, built just at the edge of the village, was held on Sept. 17, 1916; the space was consecrated on August 6 of the next year. The ceremony required for the consecration must have taken some time to arrange; three bishops of the Episcopal Church came, one account says. Miss Peterson sewed the altar cloths and curtains by hand with fine stitches. She took charge of the furnishing. She probably contributed flowers from her Gotts Island garden, just as she had for St. John the Evangelist back in Lansdowne in 1906. And she persuaded a certain number of Gotts Island Methodists to become Episcopalians.

But details are still elusive. I do not find Miss Peterson's name in the island cemetery. Nor do I see it in Philip Moore's account books. Surely, I think, Elizabeth Peterson's name was once marked on one of the postal slots that remain in the cubicle that was Philip's post office, but it has disappeared along with most of the others once visible there. I know the other names. They have a reality either etched by Philip in the handwriting learned at the business college in Bangor or carved, literally, in stone and bounded by the cemetery fence. I hear their voices, I hear the voices of my own two boys who in the 1970s were thrilled to have the remains of a real store to play in; but I cannot hear Miss Peterson's Philadelphia accents.

Voices, heard or not heard, voices heard only in memory— all are important to the story I want to tell. I hear Ben's good-bye when he set off from the Cozy Cove Restaurant in Southwest Harbor to begin the trip that would take him back to Africa; I hear his voice in the last phone conversation from Mombassa on what would turn out to be the night before he died. We cling to such memories, to all the details we have of the life that led to that savannah in East Africa. I need the details that are encapsulated in memory, there to be invoked, reworked, relived albeit in new forms. The details give me the beginning and middle of a narrative of a life. It is the ending that eludes: the fact that cannot be accommodated into what has preceded it.

So I return once again to beginnings. Ben went to Kenya because he did not want the ordinary. In his early twenties, he wanted what others might call "experience." Flying was what he loved. I expect that Miss Peterson loved Gotts Island. I see her as part of a gentle exodus, beginning in the mid-nineteenth century, of those who discovered Mount Desert Island and came back summer after summer. For some, and seemingly a proportionately large number of single women, the journey led further, out to the offshore islands. So they came, Miss Elizabeth Peterson, Miss Lucia Leffingwell, Miss Caroline Holmes. They built their houses or refurbished extant buildings, they established—as we still do—summertime relationships with the local people, and then they returned on Labor Day to homes in Philadelphia or Boston. But Miss Peterson stayed on. That was the crucial difference, the distinguishing fact. She eschewed the village that hugged the quieter, safer, western shore of the island to build her house on the rocks by the open sea— and to die in the fire that engulfed the house in the winter of 1926.

The villagers at the westerly side of the island did not even see the flames in that dark, dark, sky of a Maine winter. Vacancy marked the space between the gray house and the village. It is as if Miss Peterson's path traversed uncharted territory. We are not talking about real distance here. A mile is not far, even in bad weather on a dark night. But one mile can be like 5000. The point is that the villagers at the western side of an island that measures only "one mile across and three miles round," villagers who would soon be leaving the island permanently themselves, did not even know of the fire that took Miss Peterson's life.

I remember hearing a clock tick when I picked up the phone to receive the call that came through from Africa. It was so hard to grasp the event, to imagine both the death and its occurrence in a time zone eleven hours ahead of our own. John and I had gone to bed early. We were asleep when our son died. With the disjunction in time, the moment of the call became the reality, the moment of knowledge checked out on a clock. Time was my witness. If there were actual witnesses of that accident in Kenya, they are not mentioned in the accident report. If they exist at all, they are remote.

The witnesses to the fire that killed Miss Peterson were similarly distant: a lighthouse keeper on Great Duck Island (I cite Kenway's history here) and the men at a remote radio transmitter site at Seawall, on the mainland, who reported seeing, not the familiar light in Miss Peterson's upstairs seaward window, but sheets of flame leaping upward. Between the conflagration that took Miss Peterson's life and the witnesses lay two miles of ink-black water.

The village learned of the event the next day. I think of that moment of discovery. How different from a phone call in the night it must have been. Two Gotts Island men are on their way to neighboring Duck Island to water their sheep pastured there. It is midwinter. I imagine the cold crispness of that morning, a flint-blue sea. The men sail out of the outer pool on the village side of the island, they round Ram Island—actually a part of Gotts at low tide—and continue eastward toward Duck. They come around past the Burnham cottage, boarded and locked for the winter, and approach Miss Peterson's house on the far eastern point. They look to the tall gray house they know as a familiar landmark. And in that instant they see that the house is gone, leaving only still smoking remains and the stone foundation that is still there.

CR

The land grows over quickly on the island. In what remains of the village, we beat back the fir and spruce that try to take over our field and the scrawny remains of the Moores' orchard; stalks of brilliant fireweed cover completely what I remember as the ruins of St. Columba's, Miss Peterson's church; a neighbor has sent me a photograph of the wild flowers that appear each spring around Ben's grave. And at the other end of the island, at the rocky eastern point, Miss Peterson's once cultivated roses continue in increasing abundance their relentless march to the place where soil gives way to granite. Only the rectangle of stone remains in place, keeping watch, year after year, over the sea, dark ledges, sky.

Watching the Wind

"It is a beautiful day the wind is E. Aunt Dory is here on a visit and will go home as soon as the wind is favourable." Susanna Gott records the passing of time, wind direction, and daily events on Gotts Island with an elegant and controlled hand. In each entry, she abbreviates the directions of the compass.

The date on this occasion is May 30, 1852. Two days later the wind is a brisk N.W; and on June 11, under rather dull skies, it blows from the S.E.

On June 11 the island school children, she says, wear "garlands on [their] heads and practice calistenics [sic]." It is on this day too that Susanna first reports the dire illness of Judith Cates. "They have gone for the doctor for Miss Judith Cates," she says. "I hope medical assistance will not be in vain but I fear it will."

Throughout the summer and early fall of 1852, faithfully following the course of the wind, Susanna reports the decline and subsequent deaths of two women in the home of Captain Philip Moore: Philip's wife, Asenath Gott Moore, and Asenath's niece, the couple's adopted daughter, Judith Cates. The record does not tell us why Judith had been adopted by her aunt and uncle, or what had happened to her biological parents. Her mother was Judith Gott, Asenath's sister; we know little other than the name of her father. Judith Cates was born in December 1829. In the summer of 1852 she is twenty-two years old and an apparently permanent part of Captain Moore's household.

Mr. Harris McLean of Sullivan, Maine, descendant of two
Gotts Island families, has loaned me a copy of Susanna's
diary, an account that explains two stones in the Gotts Island cemetery. Susanna tends to tell us more about Judith,
who would have been closer to her own age. On June 15, a
dull rainy morning, the wind S.E., Susanna says that "Miss
Judith Cates seems fast failing. Mr. Moore has not yet returned with the doctor." And by the next day, foggy with
the wind gone round to the west: "Poor Judith continues to
fail the doctor has not yet arrived."

But it is not so much the illness narratives in themselves
that are so arresting; it is, rather, the conjunction between
them and the constant recording of the weather. I imagine
Susanna out each morning, reckoning the breeze. Which
way does it blow today? What is the news in this small island community? Who is coming? Who going? Who is failing, and who is dying? The wind is importantly a part of Susanna's reality, always there, a constant. Perhaps this comes
naturally to a woman living on an island where movement
on and off, to say nothing of earning a livelihood fishing
under sail, is determined in good measure by the wind. But
reading the diary one hundred fifty years later, we search
for something larger. At least in this portion of Susanna's
diary—it was to go on for several more decades—the very
constancy of the wind, in all its variations, seems ineluc-
tably connected to mortality itself. And the diarist has no
power or control over either.

As reported by Susanna, the health of both Judith and
Asenath declines precipitously in July and August 1852. On
July 7, a pleasant day with the wind southwest, we learn
that "Miss Cates is a little better," perhaps revived slightly

by the visit of her sister, Captain White's wife, from Har-
rington. But both women are described as "very low," and
Asenath is doing not well at all: "[B]leeding proceeded from
[Mrs. Moore's] mouth and not from her stomach."

The latter part of July sees a continuation of fine weather
with generally westerly breezes. It is midsummer after all.
But wind and weather, benign at this time of year, are on
the whole oblivious to the human drama taking place in
Captain Moore's house. Though Susanna might hope otherwise, there is only the feeblest connection between the
two; and the Gotts Island diarist, the faithful recorder, is
not given to extravagant hope or ill-thought judgment.

Of course we can accept the juxtaposition of weather and
health as merely the rhetorical device of a recorder for
whom weather is an essential element of existence; both
historically and culturally, Susanna's diary in fully explica-
ble in these terms. We could simply leave it at that. But still,
it is startling to encounter a mind that with such seeming
ease equates wind and mortality. We want to fill in what
appears to us a gap between elements that don't really fit.
Susanna herself is no less puzzling than her rhetoric.

Through the advancing summer, the gap between weather
and human suffering only enlarges. Susanna's language, the
events she describes, are tantalizing punctuation points in
a story whose entirety the diarist cannot really know. The
drama lies elsewhere, beneath or beyond the language. On
July 20, a beautiful morning with the wind northwest, Susanna writes that "Judith and Mrs. Moore continue very
low. Mrs. Welch has gone off to the doctor to get some
medicine," The next day, the weather remains pleasant,
the wind still northwest, but "Mrs. Moore and Judith still

continue no better." July 24 is yet another beautiful morning with the wind from the west. Susanna now dares to
think that Judith "seems a little revived by the fresh morning breeze," but in fact, "Mrs. Moore and Judith continue
about the same." And despite the little revival of July 24, by
August 8, another bright day with a good westerly wind,
Susanna reports once again that "Miss Judith is no better."
Any hope that Susanna may have for the curative powers of
a fresh morning breeze appear to be diminishing: "I wish I
could hear that she is a little revived by the fresh morning
breeze," she says.

Perhaps the sought after doctor never arrived from the
mainland; perhaps he did. The record does not tell us. We
only have Susanna's report, on another pleasant morning
with the wind once again west:

> Father commenced haying yesterday and Emily
> and I raked in the afternoon poor Mrs. Moore
> died last Thursday and was buried Saturday it
> was thought to be the largest funeral ever at-
> tended on this Island. The Cutter from Bass
> Harbor brought over a great many, and other
> boats from various places in Tremont. Rev. Mr.
> Bauker from Tremont preached the funeral
> sermon his text was Psalms 119, Uphold me
> according unto Thy word that I may live and
> let me not be ashamed of my hope. It was his
> object to describe the difference between the
> evangelical hope or the hope of the gospel and
> the false hope that fails in that day that God
> deals with them.

Mrs. Moore had died on July 29. Had "false hope" failed? Had "evangelical hope" triumphed in the end? And what of Judith, still living two months after her aunt's funeral, but failing every day? What hope did she have?

This is knowledge not available to the diarist, knowledge that wind and weather do not reveal. And surprisingly, when Judith dies in October, Susanna does not mention the event in her diary.

The two side-by-side marble stones in the Gotts Island cemetery are now the only source. Judith's is the more elaborate:

> She's gone, she's gone, the cherished one.
> Her toils are over. The victory's won.
> Just in the morning of her day.
> When hope was bright she passed away

Judith, still "in the morning of her day," still, we are told, with hope, was twenty-two years, nine months, and twenty-one days old. Asenath, whose stone reads simply "wife of Captain Philip Moore," was forty-nine years, eight months, and nineteen days old. Stones measure not wind and weather but mortal time. And they measure precisely. Captain Philip married Mary Staples Trask, a widow from neighboring Swans Island, and, as told by his stone, lived another twenty-eight years.

Susanna too lived on. The diary continues until 1910, when the handwriting is no longer controlled and elegant and the pages, at least in the version I am reading, are difficult to decipher. Susanna has now been focused for years on the drowning death of her brother William. Her diary almost obsessively records moments in the experience of loss: "This is the anniversary [of the drowning]," or, "This is his birthday," The accidental drowning death is a sudden unknowable event, not a chapter by chapter, day by day, narrative to be marked by time and wind. Nor is there a precise ending. Since William's body was never found, his family, especially his sister, were left in limbo.

Susanna is an old lady, "Aunt Sue," in the photograph Mr. McLean has sent me. Her grave is not among the many Gotts in the Gotts Island cemetery. Judith, Asenath, Philip, and Mary are all there however, buried in the row closest to the westward portion of the fence. The ground pitches sharply downward in that spot, creating pressure on the stones. Northwood Kenway has struggled to keep them straight against the slope of the hill. But the land has a will of its own, its own relationship to weather and wind. And the stones that tell the history of lives and deaths belong also to the land, to the island, to the wind.

The Art of Cemetery Maintenance

The cemetery is a real place, and like any real place on an exposed Maine island, time and merciless weather conditions take their toll. Alders and underbrush threaten the fence, which is itself subject to rot and ravage; grasses and weeds run riot; stones droop over, crack, break. It is not surprising that when Phebe Bunker made her famous trip back to the island as a ghost she found her own stone "flat as a flounder," and "tumbled over so it's hard to see the weeping willow etched on it."

But Phebe's return to the island preceded Northwood Kenway's taking responsibility for maintenance of the cemetery. Thanks to Northwood's efforts, the stones in the Gotts Island cemetery have fared much better in recent years. Northwood, whose own son lies in the cemetery, is nothing if not matter of fact about the task he has taken on. He clearly understands in the most down to earth way that preserving memory means preserving the markers in which memory is encoded. That's why his wife, Rita, includes in her book, among the histories of the island's summer families, a special section on cemetery maintenance.

Cemetery maintenance, a volunteer job at Gotts Island, makes its demands; and Northwood spells out something of what those are. Under the rubric "Monument Repair," we find Part I, "Broken Stones," and Part II, "Fallen Stones." Phebe's was a "fallen stone." In such cases, Northwood's instructions are exact: "Following directions on the product, mix an adequate quantity of Craft/Tech Floor and Wall Dry-Set Mortar with the liquid, Draft/Tech Acrylic Additive. Apply this mixed mortar with a wide putty knife to coat entirely the inside surfaces of the slot to a depth half-way from the bottom." Of such materials, with such labor, do we enable both memory and history.

Every stone in the Gotts Island cemetery now stands tall, the trunk of each weeping willow upright. The real Phebe's brothers, Berlin and Montell, are there, as are the offspring of Berlin and his wife, Blanche. We know who they are because Northwood has cleaned the stones and revealed the names once covered by lichens. He has also cleared out the spruce and alder from the fence and the enclosure, rebuilt the fence itself, and placed on the top of each upright post one of the fifty teak finials donated by a Maine native turned New Yorker who once rented our house and later died of AIDS at forty-nine. I later realized that Calvin, the donor, must have known he was dying when he contributed the finials that had been beautifully produced by a yacht-building firm in Canada. They were made, Northwood explains, to last. They were a handsome gift.

There are some seventy-five names on stones in the Gotts Island cemetery, and the number is growing. John and I are the owners of plot Number 11. I am reminded of the old song we sang as kids: "we are table number one, etc. etc." There is concreteness in these numbers.

It is one thing, and not an unusual one at that, to have a cemetery plot. It is another to have a specifically numbered plot and to have a list of all the other numbers and the still living people attached to them. At some point, all the names that now appear on the paper list will be translated to stone markers. We are all in a club that will at a still undetermined time become an organization of quite another sort. I can see who has the number 10 spot, who the 12. Northwood's inventory creates an odd sense of neighbor-

hood. While there are no house numbers on the homes of
the living at Gotts Island, there are carefully allocated plot
numbers in the village of the dead.

If I walk around the Gotts Island cemetery with Northwood's list and consult the little numbered disks on each
plot, I will see where all my island neighbors will be. But
the list, with the corresponding disks, does even more than
this. It conflates the past and the future. The small disks that
indicate the places of future denizens are juxtaposed to the
stone markers that date from the early nineteenth century
to the present, the stones that may be marble, granite, flat,
vertical, polished or rough, but all marking the islanders
already buried there. The stones mark lives once lived; the
numbered disks mark property purchased by the living.
The plot has a temporary life as a kind of real estate before
it assumes its much more permanent identity as the location of memory.

John and I purchased our little plot when Northwood told
us that the space in the cemetery was rapidly being used
up and we should sign on if we wanted to have a spot close
to Ben's grave. I think we were out on the deck having a
late afternoon drink when we saw Northwood coming up
our path to tell us this. At Gotts Island there is no moment
deemed more appropriate than another for any kind of
business, including that of cemetery plots. At any rate, we
made out the modest check that purchased us a spot, and
we received as a receipt the inclusion of our own names on
the list of everyone then enrolled. Needless to say, the list
is subject to constant change. Some people are still buying
in, and a few have moved from the paper list to their more
permanent locations.

Once on the list that gave us space in the cemetery, the issue was just where, exactly, we wanted it to be. Northwood had his yardstick with him when he appeared at our door one morning just at breakfast time. And soon, pancakes left to grow cold on the plates, we found ourselves with him down in the cemetery, measuring out the inches just to the left of Ben's simple stone. We are talking about burying ashes of course—no more full coffin burials in the small cemetery—and the plots need not be large. It was not a difficult task to measure out the rectangle that was to be assigned to us: Number 11.

We had not thought about the boundaries of the plot; we just took them for granted. Nor had we imagined that Northwood had four little disks marked number 11, one for each corner of our rectangle. I suppose that if you are in charge of a cemetery the boundaries of each measured plot are important; but strangely, I had never thought about marking them. I had imagined that perhaps one little disk would sit in the middle of our allotted space, that the boundaries would remain, at least visually, unclear. But now, I cannot avoid that imagined boundary line. We really are talking about property: a there is really there, rather uncomfortably so.

Because they are property, and at the same time much more than property, cemeteries tend to be sites of contradiction, of difficult nonmeasurables. I'm thinking of the remains of the eight Italian quarry men who drowned when the barge carrying them and the granite from nearby Black Island went down in a storm early in the last century. The details of the story are long lost, but the facts are that somewhere generally in the center of the cemetery space, unmarked, unknown, are the remains of those men. Some rough field stones once indicated their whereabouts, a neighbor tells me; but when he rehabilitated the cemetery from its unkempt state, rescuing the broken stones, repairing the old fence, and cutting away the wild brush—when he made the cemetery what it is now—Northwood removed the rough stones.

But the memory of these men cannot, should not, be forgotten. Who were these men who died in the waters just off Gotts Island? How did their bodies come to be buried there? I imagine the families in Italy who waited in vain for news of husbands, fathers, or lovers who had gone off to work in a granite quarry in far distant Maine. Could they have imagined a bleak hillside cemetery on an island overlooking the sea, a rough stone in stubbly ground? And why, one of the neighbors asked this summer, do we hear nothing of the captain of the barge that went down? How did he survive the disaster, leaving the hapless Italians to their watery fate?

These are the questions that came to mind as I stood by Ben's grave one brilliantly bright morning in late summer. Ben's stone, the modest flat oblong, seems so complete and uncomplicated. Its angles are firm. It competes with nothing. I looked at the marked off square of our plot just to the left, the four disks, each with its number 11, marking the boundaries that are so real and unreal all at the same time.

How, after all, do we measure the space of a grave, a space of memory? Even if we can speak easily of the burial plot that is so familiar, so carefully measured and numbered, cemetery maintenance comes up against imaginative and emotional understanding. Death seems too real, too know-

able. We do not want it measurable in that way. The story
of helping to measure out our own cemetery plot early one
morning is surely the stuff of small community comedy.
Later we would laugh when we told it. But the tale is too
concrete, too tight. It denies something that we do not want
to lose; it negates the power of memory that welcomes the
ambiguous, even the unreal. And because of that denial,
our laughter could not be without a hint of nervousness.

EPILOGUE: TIME TO GO

"From the time you hear the crickets it's six weeks to frost."

I hear the crickets on the island. I will not see the frost.

I know these chirping harbingers. I know the grasses drying in the field. Only a few remaining blueberries now glimmer in what was once the green, moist, and lush growth of early and midsummer. Low growing blackberries, though still red and bitter, are slowly ripening. Lustrous goldenrod begins to replace wild roses and white daisies in the field. Even the black-eyed susans are losing their vibrant yellow, nodding drowsily on their stems. The field looks and feels different, sounds different. The grasses crackle stiffly, no longer pliant. It's time to go.

"Time to Go," Ruth Moore titled the poem where she and Uncle Mont Gott witness the looming. It's a poem that figures the final departure of the islanders. In terms of such leavetakings, the end of another summer on the island is considerably less dramatic, its scale hardly comparable. Ruth looked out to fantasy islands looming far to the westward. Coming down the path for the last time of this summer, bags in hand, I want to turn and look east, to see the field glistening with the early morning dew and the house still lightly shrouded in mist against the slowly mounting sun.

The work of cleaning, packing up, organizing, and arranging has been done, and we are on our way. "Don't look back yet," I tell myself. I'm following the path across the Kenways' yard, heading toward the cemetery. Only there, at the small granite rectangle of Ben's grave, can I allow myself to look back and follow, yet again, the line of sight to the house that sits high on its hill.

Ruth Moore wrote another poem about a very different leavetaking, a piece addressed ostensibly to summer but perhaps to a lost love or even to a passing chapter in her life. "Mountain of Snow—1934" is a sadder, even bitter, farewell. Here are "rocks that will never miss you," "pitiless water and impassive air." "Compassionate" summer days are only "leased" to us, "less than smoke, / Less than a flight of sparrows in the air." Diamond dew in the grasses and mist-shrouded forms turning to gold in the morning light have no place in a "flinty" landscape where another spring is marked only by "Daisy and everlasting, saxifrage, /The slow, reluctant blooming out of stone."

If I have never seen the frost, neither have I seen that blooming out of stone that signals the coming of spring on the island. But stone may bloom in other ways. On this still morning in late summer with sounds of fall already in the air, a scattering of miniature petals adorns the stone adjacent to Ben's. The daughter of another summer family, her life also tragically cut short in a fatal accident, is buried here. Her stone, flat and simple like Ben's, is decorated today with the petals of daisies, black-eyed susans, and blackberry blossoms, all arranged in a delicate pattern against the pale granite and simple Roman lettering. In this blooming, a family, in an act of love, marks its loss.

Then, suddenly, the air stirs, breaking the stillness of the morning. With the light breeze, the tiny petals scatter like confetti into the surrounding grasses. A special moment has passed.

But the island has left us a gift. Our simple ritual of farewell that signals the end of another island summer has been altered. The memory picture now includes tiny bright petals on the ground around the cemetery stones. Here too are harbingers. The petals tell us that despite the stark New England climate where spring returns only with "reluctance," the wild flowers will defy the "wild wet winds" and win the struggle to bloom "out of stone." The lupine, roses, daisies, and blueberries will all be back. And with bags, bundles, and memory, so will we.

AN ESSAY ON SOURCES

No book, no work of place or memory, stands alone. A number of sources and a number of writers, past and present, have been particularly important in helping me "see" Gotts Island and produce my own vision. Most of these works are cited directly in my book, some not, but I am indebted to them all: Eliot Porter's *Summer Island*; John Fowles's *Islands*; Philip Conkling's *Islands in Time*; David Platt and Philip Conkling's *Holding Ground: The Best of Island Journal*; George Putz's "A Singular Community" in the *Holding Ground* volume; Greg Dening's *Beach Crossings: Voyaging Across Times, Cultures, and Self*; John Gillis's *Islands of the Mind*; Charles B. McLane's *Islands of the Mid-Maine Coast: Blue Hill and Penobscot Bays*; H. W. Small's, *History of Swan's Island*; and Sarah Orne Jewett's *Country of the Pointed Firs and Other Stories*.

I am not the first writer to be inspired by Gotts Island. My book owes much, first, to Ruth Moore for her fiction, especially *The Weir* and *Speak to the Winds*, and for her poetic vision in *The Tired Apple Tree* and *Time's Web*; to Sanford Phippen for *High Clouds Soaring, Storms Driving Low: The Letters of Ruth Moore*; to Katherine Crosby, "Mystery of Gotts Island" (in the *Boston Globe*); to Harris McLean for the unpublished diary of Susanna Gott; and particularly important, to Rita Kenway, who researched the history of the island and chronicled its families in *Gotts Island and Its People*.

Some books speak particularly to the concerns of my book. Here I am indebted to Rebecca Solnit for *A Field Guide to Getting Lost*, *Wanderlust*, and *A Book of Migrations*; to Susan Stewart for *On Longing: Narratives of the Miniature, the Gigantic, the Souvenir, the Collection*; to Sandra Gilbert for her critical study, *Death's Door: Modern Dying and the Ways We Grieve*, and for her poems collected in *Belongings*; to Gary Laderman for *The Sacred Remains: American Attitudes Toward Death, 1799–1883*; to Frances Yates for her classic work on memory in the rhetorical tradition, *The Art of Memory*; to Robin Jaffee Frank for *Love and Loss: American Portrait and Mourning Miniatures*; to Robin Jarvis for *Romantic Writing and Pedestrian Travel*; to Akiko Busch for *Geography of Home*; and to Amy Willard Cross for *Summer House: A Tradition of Leisure*.